One True Home

Behind the Veil of Forgetfulness

Claire Candy Hough

To Heather,

Love and Angel Blessings,

Candy

ANGEL HEALING HOUSE

LOS ANGELES, CA

ONE TRUE HOME
Claire Candy Hough

ISBN 13: 978-0-9818576-1-9
ISBN 10: 0-9818576-1-2

Printed in the U.S.A.

First U.S. Edition: 2015

Library of Congress Control Number: 2015943115

Published by
Angel Healing House
Los Angeles, California

www.angelhealinghouse.com

Dedication

I am eternally grateful and more appreciative than I could ever express to my Archangels, brother and sister Angels, and my spirit guides. This group, who I affectionately call 'The Posse of Angels,' has always been around me and never left my side. They have lovingly guided, protected and watched over me with enormous care, concern and vigilance.

Thank you for being there to celebrate my triumphs, thank you for your compassion and showing me the light when life became dark and I lost hope.

Thank you for your constant support and ever-present reminder of how to shine forth my Divine eternal nature.

I love you all so dearly.

Acknowledgements

I would like to express my deep appreciation for my parents, Leonard and Sylvia Milgraum. Your constant support for me to be true to myself and to keep following my dreams has been a beacon of light for me to follow. I was very clever when I chose you both to be my parents.

I also owe a great debt of gratitude to my beautiful mother-in-law, Olga Hough. She provided a safe, protective haven for my husband and me to live while we were waiting for my husband Pete's green card to be finalized in Australia. When our plans to move to the States were held up after selling our house, she compassionately opened up her heart to help us without a moment of hesitation. Her kindness over those five months enabled me to put all my focus and attention on channeling this beautiful book, *One True Home*. She is an angel on the Earth plane and I am eternally grateful.

To my beloved Twin Flame, Pete: Thank you for always treating me like your precious Princess and encouraging me to spread my angel's wings and fly.

And finally, thank you to Patricia and Joyce of Park Place Publications, and George of Foster Covers for their help in bringing this book together.

Preface

I speak to my Grandmother Sarah every day. Her loving, supportive, caring and no-nonsense advice has helped me through countless hardships and provided me with her unique blend of wise insights. I don't know where I would have been these past fifty years without her deep devotion to my happiness and wellbeing.

My Grandmother Sarah is my guardian angel and she died when I was eight years old. I hear her voice and smell her lilac perfume when she comes to call. To verify that it is she, my Grandmother Sarah shows me a vision of some sort of traditional Jewish fare. I figured out long ago that by presenting me with a noodle dish or a delicious trifle, she was encouraging me to eat more; as she thinks I am too skinny. (God bless you Grandma!)

Although she has passed from physical life, she is every bit as intelligent, kind, loving and determined now that she resides in her 'True Home.'

The fact that I speak to her every day is neither unusual nor strange for me. The difference between me and the many people who don't hear the voices of loved ones who have crossed over from the physical to the non-physical, is that they are choosing not to listen.

The idea of our Divine eternal nature is nothing new and has been written about and debated throughout time.

One of the more prominent people who believed that our Spirit is eternal was renowned scientist Benjamin Franklin, who wrote:

"When I see nothing annihilated (in the works of God) and not a drop of water wasted, I cannot suspect the annihilation of souls, or believe that He will suffer the daily waste of millions of minds ready made that now exist, and put Himself to the continual trouble of making new ones. Thus, finding myself to exist in the world, I believe I shall, in some shape or other, always exist; and, with all the inconveniences human life is liable to, I shall not object to a new edition of mine, hoping, however that the errata of the last may be corrected."

And just as reincarnation and the concept of our soul always existing was Benjamin Franklin's truth; it is my truth as well.

I have always felt this profound connection with Spirit and it was made stronger with my two near-death experiences.

One True Home is based on the true story of my past lives and my experiences between those lives, as each incarnation was a precious step along the path toward my spiritual awakening and self-realization.

By recounting my incarnations and my journey back to our '*One True Home*,' I hope it will open others to the awareness of the limitless and boundless Divine eternal potential that is inside each and every one of us.

Perhaps Benjamin Franklin's epitaph, which he wrote himself, says it best:

The Body of
B. Franklin, Printer;
Like the Cover of an old Book,
Its Contents torn out,
And stript of its Lettering and Gilding,
Lies here, Food for Worms.
But the Work shall not be wholly lost:
For it will, as he believ'd, appear once more,
In a new & more perfect Edition,
Corrected and amended
By the Author.

I wish you well on the extraordinary journey that we all get to take as we travel back to our '*One True Home*.'

Love and Angel Blessings,
Claire Candy Hough

Chapters

One True Home

Behind the Veil of Forgetfulness

1

Giza, Egypt, 2560 B.C.

The pregnant full moon guided the Egyptian barge over the mirror-like surface of the River Nile. Although the hot summer sun had vanished from the sky hours ago, the warmth of the day lingered in the calm of the evening. Traveling at night not only meant cooler temperatures at this time of the year, but it allowed greater security for the precious cargo on board. When a vessel was entrusted with this kind of wealth, great precautions were taken to assure its safe arrival.

The massive armed guards aboard the vessel stood watch while carefully scanning the illuminated river bank for any signs of trouble. Not only had these muscular men been screened and selected for their prowess as skilled warriors, they had something else in common. They were all eunuchs.

This was the royal barge that had been summoned to carry the next wife of the Pharaoh to her new home in Alexandria. Its heavy gold ornamentation and lavish inlaid mother-of-pearl sparkled as it caught the reflection of the silvery moon.

Gliding silently through the waters, the vessel ever so gently folded back the waves as if one were folding back bolts of delicate silk. The helmsman was ordered to keep the vessel's journey smooth and without incident. In this way it would allow for an excited yet sleepy Princess to reach her destination fully refreshed. But sleep was the furthest thing from the Princess's mind.

Nestled in the enclosed cabin on board, Ankhesenamun lay on a soft bed surrounded by pillows of embroidered silk. She had been feeling a sense of trepidation, unable to sleep for hours. It was strange that she should feel uneasy; as this journey was something that she had been primed for ever since she could remember. Her mind drifted back as she recalled the meeting with her intended thirteen years earlier.

Summoned from her play by her parents, the three-year-old Princess was introduced to a tall, handsome man. At thirty-five years of age, Akhenaten had been newly crowned Pharaoh upon the recent death of his father.

Sitting in the gardens amidst the fruit-laden date palms and the colorful peacocks, the Pharaoh asked the Princess questions as he listened intently to her answers. The little Princess noticed a deep scar etched into his right cheek and asked him what had happened.

He told her of his courage in killing the lion that had inflicted his wound. Without hesitation and with childlike innocence, she tenderly ran her finger over the scar. The Pharaoh was so touched by her compassionate action that he would later tell her parents it was this one, loving gesture from one so young that convinced him of her pure heart and worthiness to be crowned his wife one day.

From that day forward, she was taught, groomed and instructed on how to be a Queen. It came as no surprise when the announcement was finally made that she would go forth to marry, leaving the only family she had ever known.

Confused, Ankhesenamun wondered what was causing this uneasiness in her youthful heart. Peering through the slats of her cabin, she noticed the first rays of sunlight appearing on the horizon. The increased sounds on board alerted her that they would soon anchor at their destination. Ankhesenamun noticed that a small boat glided through the water toward her vessel and was favorably met by her guards.

These were the handmaidens sent to prepare the Princess for her meeting with the Pharaoh. Carrying bolts of silk, the handmaidens entered the cabin and began to bathe and dress the Princess. They draped her in many different colors of materials to determine the exact hue that would enhance her beauty. Finally, an exquisite pale pink silk was chosen to best compliment her olive skin.

The handmaidens worked in silent deference to one who was so much higher in rank than their lowly station. With a minimum of both movement and expression, they deftly applied her makeup and crimson lips. The dark kohl pencil expertly applied made Ankhesenamun's huge brown eyes seem even larger.

To complete the outfit, the last accessory was placed over her head and rested upon her youthful chest. Looking down at the bejeweled ceremonial necklace, the Princess recognized many of the rare gemstones and crystals. As part of her grooming to be Pharaoh's wife, she had been well taught on the characteristics and powers of these precious stones. Purple amethysts assured the wearer of protection, dispelled negativity and promoted spiritual awareness. The powerful rainbow moonstone, emanating its milky bluish and white hues, was said to enhance feminine qualities and help with fertility and childbirth. The soft pale pink of rose quartz encouraged the compassionate emotion of love. And the sun-like yellow of the gemstone citrine brought prosperity, wealth and abundance to the wearer.

With her outfit complete, Ankhesenamun stepped out of her cabin on to the deck. Looking behind her, she glanced at the second barge that had followed them. This barge was filled with the Princess's dowry and its hold was overflowing with gold, silver and precious jewels. The Princess believed that marriage to a Pharaoh was a great honor, allowing her family lifelong protection and security. For in those days, it was more important who you knew than the wealth you had acquired. A family's connection was of the utmost importance in uncertain times.

Having reached the shore, she climbed onto an enclosed litter draped in material. The cloth surrounding the litter not only sheltered the rider from the searing heat of the sun and dust from swirling desert sands, it also served to hide the identity of the occupant.

Six of her enormous guards easily picked up the litter, hoisted the poles upon their shoulders and walked in unison on the journey to the palace of the Pharaoh. The combination of the swaying of the litter, the increasing heat and weariness quickly lulled the Princess to sleep.

All of a sudden, she was startled awake by what seemed like thunder. As her eyes adjusted, she saw in the distance a hazy wash of color and heard an increasing sound of cheering voices coming from the crowds who had been summoned to welcome her arrival.

Approaching the steps of the palace, the guards gently lowered the Princess to the ground. Surprised by the enormity of the crowds, the Princess was glad to hide behind the veil secured over her face. Climbing down, she felt her heart beating faster than hummingbird's wings as she was lead up the steps to the palace.

As Ankhesenamun arrived at the top of the steps, a procession of the Pharaoh's Council gathered around her. A group of beautifully dressed women of various ages stood behind them. Their exquisite embroidered gowns and ornate headdresses denoted women of high position. The Princess surmised that perhaps these elegantly dressed women were the Pharaoh's mother, aunts and sisters.

A ram's horn sounded and the Council parted, revealing an old, overweight man who approached her. Taking her small, delicate hands in his oversized, wrinkled palms, the old man said how pleased he was for her arrival. She immediately winced and gasped for air as she smelled the foul stench of his breath; a result of his decaying teeth. It was then that she noticed the familiar deep scar on the right side of his face.

Holding up her hand, he said, "This is my new wife and your future Queen. Ankhesenamun and I ask the gods to bless our upcoming union."

A feeling of utter dread came over the Princess. She recognized the same man she had been introduced to thirteen years earlier. Yet now, with ill health, his once handsome, virile body had grown portly and had started to decline.

The Pharaoh summoned the group of women forward and introduced his four existing wives to the Princess. Bowing out of respect, their expressionless faces stoically acknowledged her. At no stage was the Princess ever told that the Pharaoh would have more than one wife. As the aging Pharaoh's health had deteriorated over time, he hoped to regain his health by taking a new, younger queen to bring back his strength and virility.

Wanting desperately to run home to the comfort of her mother's arms, Ankhesenamun bit her lip so hard that she could taste blood. Carried along by the great cheers of the crowd, she was lead to her royal chamber. It was only when she was finally left alone that she allowed her shock and sadness to pour out of her. Heavy tears caused dark streaks of kohl eye pencil to stream down her beautiful face.

As she prayed to be rescued by the gods, her worn-out body gave way to exhaustion and her prayers were answered in the form of a blessed blanket of sleep.

The first rays of the morning sun filtered through the curtains around her bed. The song of a little bird on her balcony made the Princess stir. She felt the warmth of her mother's loving arms holding fast around her shoulders as they sat together in their family's lush garden.

Looking deeply into her daughter's eyes, her mother said, "We love you and if the gods allow, we will all be together again soon." Her mother stood up, kissed her daughter and slowly her silhouette began to fade away. Desperately reaching out to recapture her mother's hand, the Princess heard her soothing voice, "Be strong my child and make us proud of you."

Awakening from the dream, Ankhesenamun slowly opened her eyes. Remembering that the palace was now her new home, she was filled with dread, and big tears started to form again in her sad, swollen eyes. Her anguish was interrupted as she was startled by a loud knock at the door.

A handmaiden entered balancing a water vessel on top of her head. Gracefully bending over, she filled a basin with water and some rose petals. Without uttering a single word, she silently washed away the dark circles under the Princess's eyes.

The handmaiden's gentle and tender touch conveyed that this was not the first time that she had comforted a frightened, young Princess. As the handmaiden put her hand into the perfumed water, Ankhesenamun reached in and touched her hand.

"Thank you for caring. What is your name?"

Shocked and surprised, the handmaiden had never been spoken to in such a kind manner. Hesitantly looking up, her voice trembled. "My name is Maat."

The Princess asked her to speak about her life. Maat's birth had been a result of one of the Pharaoh's many encounters with the slave girls in the palace. She was from a long line of handmaidens to the royal family and her entire life had been spent in servitude.

Although the two girls could not have been more diametrically opposed in social ranking, they had an instant inner feeling of compassion toward each other's plight. Sitting together on the side of the Princess's bed, their conversation flowed easily. After a short time, it became quite apparent that they had more in common than they would have ever imagined.

They spoke openly about the dreams, hopes and wishes of all young girls on the verge of experiencing womanhood. Having expressed her fears and sorrow about her upcoming union with the decaying Pharaoh, Ankhesenamun felt as if a heavy burden had been lifted off her youthful shoulders.

Their conversation was interrupted by a messenger's announcement that the Princess was summoned to appear before the Council. The girls gave each other a knowing smile, having found a confidante and a kindred spirit.

Entering a large stone arena, the Princess descended a flight of steps into a circular pit. The Pharaoh's Council was positioned in stadium-like seating and looked down on her from above. In this way, the Council towered over anyone before them, demonstrating their superiority and making the person feel small and insignificant.

This meeting was to brief the Princess on the likes and dislikes of the Pharaoh. She was also informed of the ranking of the Pharaoh's wives and how they should be treated accordingly. The Council explained that, even with her royal status, there would be unpleasant consequences if these orders were not obeyed.

With her spirit all but broken, the resignation showed in her stooped shoulders and lifeless expression. Lastly, the Council told her that the union to the Pharaoh would be postponed until the following month. This waiting period was necessary, as it allowed time for the detection of any diseases that the Princess may have brought with her. In this way, the Pharaoh's life would not be placed in jeopardy. It was for this reason that she was to remain in isolation from all members of the royal family.

On this announcement, the light came back into Ankhesenamun's face. She breathed a huge sigh of relief, realizing that she would have a month's reprieve from her terrible fate.

Over those initial days of life in the palace, the Princess resigned herself to the opulent, yet isolated surroundings. As a reminder that the Pharaoh had not forgotten about their upcoming union, he sent her daily gifts of jewelry and trinkets. Rather than lightening her sadness, these gifts only served as a harsh reminder of what was to come. She would have gladly given away these lavish gifts and the honor of marrying a Pharaoh for a chance to return home to her family once more. Her forced isolation made her grateful for her friendship with Maat.

As their friendship grew, Maat divulged that she was in love with a sweet young man who also was in service to the Pharaoh. By palace law, it was strictly forbidden for any servants to have relations with one other. It was then that she told the Princess of their hope to one day run away from their life of slavery and to marry.

Not long after her conversation with Maat, Ankhesenamun sat in the quiet of her private garden. After a short while, the silence was slowly taken over by a sweet sound of music played on a lyre. The delicate, soft notes spoke so tenderly to her heart that she was curious to see who was playing the instrument. Standing on a garden bench, she peered over the wall and was able to view an open courtyard. Fragrant flowers of jasmine and frangipani surrounded a cascading fountain. The flowers' perfumed scents wafted on the delicate spray churned up by the tumbling waters.

Perched on the side of the fountain was a curly-haired musician. It was obvious that he was well skilled in the art of playing the lyre, as his fingers glided over the strings with great sensitivity. Listening to the dulcet tones, Ankhesenamun stood, silently captivated by his playing. As the musician completed the final chord of his song, the Princess applauded loudly.

Surprised, the young man looked around for the face of his enthusiastic admirer and was just able to discern the top of a head and eyes peering over the wall. Jumping up on the edge of the fountain, the young man was stunned by the Princess's appearance, and he bowed low. Praising him for his wonderful playing, the Princess asked his name and inquired whether he could teach her how to play. He said his name was Amun and that he would be honored to give her lessons.

From that day on, Amun gave Ankhesenamun daily instructions on how to play the lyre. No matter how many mistakes the Princess made, he would patiently correct her. The music lessons were a welcomed distraction and brought back some joy into the Princess's life.

In the weeks that followed, Ankhesenamun was not surprised to learn that it was Amun who Maat loved. Having to hide behind the secrecy of their love, they prayed for the day when they could be together. When Maat spoke of Amun, her voice contained such sweet adoration for her beloved that it made the Princess yearn even more for the life of true love, which would always be denied her.

It was this yearning in her desperate heart that prompted the

Princess to ask Maat to help her escape from the palace as she could not bear to be wed to the old Pharaoh.

Three days before her wedding day, the Princess asked Maat to hide a servant's dress among the towels for her daily bath. Dressing as a handmaiden with a headdress and veil to hide her appearance, Ankhesenamun waited until the hallway outside her room was empty.

For the past month, the Princess had noticed that the guards outside her door were not very attentive to their positions. Having fought valiantly in many strategic battles, these warriors considered this appointment of watching over a young girl well beneath their military status. Their attitude was reflected in their half-hearted attempts and they were not always present at their posts outside her door.

The girls decided to wait until after the Princess's evening meal before their escape. In this way, it would have been accepted for Ankhesenamun not to be seen again until the light of morning. As the last rays of the late afternoon sun streamed across her balcony, the Princess prayed to the gods for an easy escape. Creeping out into the empty hallway, the two veiled girls quickly made their way outside and hurried out of the palace gates into an open public arena.

Maat knew that tonight was the start of a three day market held every month. Stall holders had arrived throughout the day from far and wide setting up their tents. Once the glaring sun went down, the cool of the evening temperatures allowed for old friends to get together and visit. The commotion and the noise was deafening to Ankhesenamun's ears. In her sheltered, protected life of privilege, she had never experienced anything like this before.

Frozen still like a terrified fawn, she stood mesmerized by the chaotic scene. The exotic aromas from the cooking stalls mingled with the smells of the camels and goats. The squawking chickens in their cages seemed to be competing for attention from the colorful street performers, musicians and belly dancers.

A sharp tug on her sleeve quickly diverted the Princess's attention away from the mayhem as Maat signaled for her to follow. Stepping carefully between the snake charmers and the jugglers, they made their way down a crowded alleyway.

Approaching a small, disheveled house, Maat and Ankhesenamun pushed open its weathered door. Firmly closing it behind them, Maat moved a rug and revealed a hidden hatch within the floor. Gently lifting the door, the girls made their way down a secret flight of steps. Entering the underground level of the house, the girls saw an old man and woman silently weaving baskets. As the couple looked up, they smiled and Maat went over to kiss them both.

As the old woman poured some water for the girls, she asked Maat if she was all right, and reached across to touch her stomach.

"Thank you, I am fine," replied Maat. "But this little one won't stay little for long. I am just starting to show now. That's why it's so important that we must escape tonight." Noticing Ankhesenamun's questioning gaze, Maat quickly said, "It is Amun's, not the Pharaoh's."

Their conversation was suddenly cut short with the noise of heavy footsteps on the floor above. They watched cautiously as Amun's curly mop of hair popped through the door and Maat's face beamed. Away from the palace restrictions, the lovers fell in each other's arms and embraced fully. Placing a loving hand on his mother's shoulder, Amun asked how she was.

"I am well, my son. Your brother will be leaving before sunrise tomorrow to cut stone at the quarry. In preparation for the three day journey, the carts were loaded this afternoon. You will need to be hidden on them tonight."

Kissing his mother goodbye, Amun had an awful feeling in his heart. The old woman bowed her head and prayed to the gods to bless her family with a safe passage. Under cover of darkness, Amun, Maat and Ankhesenamun crept quietly to stow away amongst the provisions in the heavily-laden carts. Hidden under rugs and sacks of flour, it didn't take long before all three brave souls fell into an exhaustive sleep.

It took the Pharaoh's guards only twenty-four hours to find the

Princess and her young accomplices. The Pharaoh had many spies who were more than eager to receive extra rations and privileges for certain information. The heavy-handed guards bound the arms of the three youths and threw them into the back of a cart.

As they approached the city walls, Amun gasped in horror as they saw the severed heads of both his mother and father on top of poles outside the palace gates. This was a very persuasive warning to all others who may have entertained thoughts about being an accomplice to disobeying royal orders. The Pharaoh never lost an opportunity to demonstrate the power and control of his position and had summoned all his people to assemble at the palace.

Bound securely by ropes, Amun and Maat were pushed up the steps as the Pharaoh addressed his people.

"I will not tolerate disobedience from anyone. There can only be one outcome if one chooses to disobey me."

Trembling, the lovers were made to stand facing each other and an executioner stood behind each of them. They then watched in helpless horror as their beloved was simultaneously beheaded. Although Ankhesenamun was not at the scene, she was forced to watch the event from the balcony of a secluded room in the palace.

It was easy disposing of the two slaves. After all, the Pharaoh had so many servants, what did it matter if he made a public example of two more? But, the issue of the disobedient Princess was of greater concern to him. If he killed her publically, the news would get back to her parents and the rich alliance that they had forged with the Pharaoh would be broken. Yet, if it were made public that the Princess did not want to marry the Pharaoh because he was old and ill, it would lead to great shame and humiliation.

The next morning, two huge guards burst into her room, abruptly awakening Ankhesenamun. Grabbing the Princess, the guards forcefully dragged her into the great stone arena of the Pharaoh's Council. Binding her hands and legs, the guards threw her into the pit. Summoned to stand up, she wearily rose to her feet. The Pharaoh then entered the arena and sat down; his expressionless face did not look directly at Ankhesenamun, but gazed off into the distance. The oldest of the Council members stepped forward, unrolled a scroll and read aloud.

"To the loving parents of Ankhesenamun, I am very sorry to tell you that, soon after your daughter and I were wed, she fell ill to disease. Fortunately we were able to quarantine her in time and the Royal family was not affected. Unfortunately, her condition became worse and I am sad to inform you that your daughter has died. We are sorry for your loss."

Having conveyed to her parents that the contractual part of the marriage agreement was dutifully followed, the Pharaoh knew that he could keep the riches from her dowry.

As the Princess's bruised and exhausted body tried to digest the enormity of what she was just told, she watched one of the Council members reach for a large pole hanging on the wall. He leaned over the side of the pit and slipped the end of the pole into a tiny latch near the floor. Unhooking the latch, a small door was freed and swung open as all eyes of the Council were riveted on the tiny opening.

A few moments later, a snake peered around the corner and was pushed through the door. The Princess looked on in horror as the snake made its way around the edge of the pit. Soon, more poisonous cobras and vipers were pushed through the door. Their aggressive natures were immediately heightened, and they reared up and started to strike. In anticipation of the inevitable, several Council members appeared on various sides of the pit to get a closer look.

The Princess kept to the middle of the circle and continually tried to avoid the deadly snakes. She prayed to the gods to quickly take her away. Suddenly, a cobra struck her on the ankle and she could feel the heat and burning pain from the venom course through her veins. Waiting for death to overcome her, she closed her eyes, took a deep breath in and ….

2

Heaven – The Journey Back Home
We All Get To Take

… Immediately, the searing pain from the snake bite was gone. The Princess slowly opened her eyes and strangely found herself looking down on the Council from above. She winced as she saw herself in the pit, still covered with a writhing mound of snakes. While trying to make sense of her confusion, she heard a Scottish voice come out of thin air.

"I used to have a terrible fear of snakes meself." Immediately, the air started to take form and shaped itself into a tall, lovely young girl with flowing red hair. Floating casually next to Ankhesenamun, the young girl continued, "Aye, me name is Ainslie; I have come to take you home. You no longer have to worry about snakes anymore or anythin' else for that matter."

Forgetting about her confusion, Ankhesenamun focused on a possible escape. "Let's go quickly before the Council sees us." Taking Ainslie's hand, the Princess felt a pull as her whole body was sucked into a cave. Although strange at first, there was something vaguely familiar in the sensation of being in this dark place. The Princess surmised that Ainslie was a sorceress that the gods had sent to hide her in this black cave. A bright white light appeared off in the distance and she became aware of a whooshing sound as she and Ainslie were lifted up and began to float towards the light.

As her eyes adjusted to the darkness within the cave, the Princess became aware of her surroundings, and was surprised to see that she and Ainslie were not alone. This cave was very large with plenty of room as she saw many men, women and children also floating towards the light. It made her laugh as she saw not only people but many different types of animals calmly floating to the light as well.

It dawned on her that she was no longer worried about the snakes, the Council, the Pharaoh or anything else for that matter. Actually, she felt rather peaceful and calm, with a complete knowing in her heart that everything was going to be all right. As an unseen force pulled her along, the cave began to lighten as the opening drew closer.

Focusing on the opening of the cave, the Princess was just able to distinguish that there were people waiting outside. As she came closer to them, she was amazed when she saw her Aunt Banafrit and her Grandfather Mhotep smiling and waving at her.

"How is it possible that they are here? They both died when I was a child?"

"We are traveling to our real home where nobody ever dies. Your loved ones have come to greet you with a homecomin' party."

In shock, the Princess tried to make sense of what was happening. With a huge smile on her face, she declared loudly, "So this is what the afterlife looks like!"

Stepping out of the tunnel, the Princess recognized many familiar loved ones who had crossed over into the afterlife, yet were welcoming her back home. Out of everyone whom she reconnected with, she cried most of all when she saw Maat and Amun walk towards her. Fully restored to health and wholeness, Maat's arms were wrapped around the beautiful baby girl that she had conceived. The three young friends hugged each other with great joy as they were reunited once again.

Startled, the Princess felt something cold and wet on her leg. Looking down, she saw her beloved little dog, Nubia, which had died when she was twelve. Gleefully scooping the little dog up in her arms, she nuzzled her and swung her around in a circle. The feeling of love in her heart was overwhelming.

For the first time since stepping into the light, she gazed around and gave full attention to her new surroundings. The Princess was astonished as she recognized that she was in the middle of her family's beautiful garden. Every minute detail, from the abundant fruit-laden trees that had provided shade for the garden's carved marble benches, to the sparkling fountain surrounded by the purple lilac trees and shrieking peacocks, was an exact replica of her beloved home.

It suddenly dawned on her that this might be another dream.

Walking over to the flowers circling the fountain, the Princess pulled off a petal and touched it to her cheek. It felt very real as it was soft and delicate and the fragrance filled her senses. Turning to her guide, she hesitantly said in a shaky voice, "Ainslie, is this just another dream? Will I awaken to be married to the Pharaoh?"

"No my dear," Ainslie replied in a caring, loving voice. "This is reality. The life you just came from was the dream."

Smiling with relief, the Princess sat down on a stone bench in her wonderful garden and was joyously reacquainted with her loved ones.

After some time, Ainslie approached the Princess. Holding out her hand to Ankhesenamun, she said, "It is now time to come with me for your orientation process to begin." Sensing the Princess's hesitation and sadness, Ainslie continued, "You can revisit your loved ones anytime you want. They are merely a thought form away."

"What do you mean?" the Princess replied with a quizzical look on her face.

"Come, I'll explain it to you as we walk along."

The path was lined with lilac trees as they passed beautiful beings of light who smiled and waved at them.

"Who are they?" said the Princess.

"Those beings are gentle souls called angels. They were carefully selected by God to be compassionate hosts to welcome back those people who cross over into the afterlife. They help reunite people with their loved ones." Glancing over at the Princess, Ainslie confirmed, "Aye, you're right; I am an angel too."

Startled, the Princess said, "How did you know what I was thinking?"

"Well, that's easy," said Ainslie. "Everyone is telepathic and psychic in Heaven. As a matt'r of fact, this is one of the abilities that we, in Heaven, share with those on Earth."

"We were told that only the wise Shaman has the ability of foresight," the Princess quickly replied, "and that to practice it was evil."

Ainslie rolled her eyes and tossed her red hair. "Most Earth people stop others from practicing their intuitive powers because they want to have control over them and they do not wish for them to have independent thoughts. Regardless of this, most people have forgotten their psychic abilities because they have forgotten their Divine eternal natures and their connection to God."

Tears started to form in the Princess's eyes as her soul started to remember the feeling of utter bliss and reconnection to the Divine that is every soul's birthright to experience.

Ainslie continued, "Unlike the Earth plane, we do not hide our thoughts from one another, for there is nothing to hide. There is no greed, no jealousy, no prejudice, no competition, no envy nor anger here. We are all love. We are all one. We live and work together for the betterment of all. We have nothing to hide or to be ashamed of, so why should we keep our thoughts secret?"

Stopping briefly along the path, Ainslie put her nose into a large gardenia and breathed deeply. "In Heaven, our use of creative thought can only be used for good intentions and only positive thoughts will materialize. No matter how hard someone tries, negative thoughts will not be able to be generated. You see, Princess, everything in Heaven is created by thought. Everyone here has the ability to manifest whatever they want for themselves, just by thinking about it. You can create what kind of house you reside in, the clothes you would like to wear and anything else that you would like to have. You can even choose to appear differently. Watch, I'll show you."

Ainslie's long, wavy, red hair turned black, short and straight. She went from being very tall to being very short. She then changed her fair white complexion to dark brown.

The Princess was astonished. "Doesn't this confuse people?"

Reversing her appearance once again, Ainslie smiled. "In Heaven, we have the ability to know a person by their inner light, which never changes regardless of their outward appearance."

The winding path that they had been walking along abruptly ended. In front of them appeared a magnificent Grecian building adorned with ornately carved columns. The Princess saw huge rose pink marble steps ascending to massive doors of gold. "What building is this?"

"This is the Hall of Justice," Ainslie replied, "where all souls go after they have completed a life on Earth."

She explained that all souls in Heaven are given the choice to attend Earth or not. And while it is in no way compulsory or looked down upon if one chooses not to go, there are definite limitations to one's spiritual growth for those who choose not to experience life on Earth.

The Princess was puzzled. "How do we know where to go and what family to choose when we return to Earth?"

Even though Ainslie had given this same explanation countless times before, she lovingly delivered it as if it were for the very first time. "You see, dear Princess, each time we choose to descend to Earth, we have asked for certain lessons and challenges to be part of our journey in life. We experience and learn from them in order to grow spiritually. It may come as a surprise, but whatever lesson a person chooses is totally up to them. In this way, the person will hopefully learn from the challenges that they have created for themselves to experience."

Looking up at the top of the marbled steps, both Ainslie and the Princess saw that the doors started to glow brightly. Ainslie smiled. "All is ready for you now, and it's your turn to enter the Hall of Justice." Seeing that the Princess was waiting for Ainslie to walk with her, Ainslie laughed. "Every person has to review their life on their own, in the presence of God. But don't worry, when the review is over, I will be here awaitin' for you."

As the Princess walked up the pink marble steps, the massive golden doors slowly began to swing open. Walking into a large open area, the Princess felt a familiar sense that she had been here before. The hall in which she stood was enormous and had a beautiful domed ceiling. In the middle of the hall was a single marble bench, and she instinctively knew to sit down.

A three-dimensional screen appeared and began to show the Princess the incarnation that she had just lived from her birth until her death by snake bite. While watching her life, she experienced what others felt as a result of her actions. And while she was proud of her considerate and loving gestures, she also experienced the pain that her judgmental, deceitful and hateful choices caused others. Throughout the whole screening, there were no feelings of rejection, judgment or even being criticized. However, the Princess did experience an overwhelming sense of joy from God that she had chosen to complete a physical life on Earth.

After her life review, the Princess left the Hall of Justice. Waiting for her at the bottom of the steps was Ainslie. Having done this countless time before, the angel gently took the Princess's hand and led her in silence towards the Hall of Akashic Records. Ainslie knew that souls are usually very quiet and reflective after viewing their lives and she had learned to honor their quiet contemplation.

Walking further along the path, they soon came to another massive building. Mirroring the Hall of Justice, this beautiful structure was also constructed of the palest pink marble. Its highly polished sheen reflected wonderful prisms of light and gave the whole building a glow of soft radiance.

Sensing another of Ankhesenamun's questions, Ainslie answered the Princess before she could ask it. "The Hall of Akashic Records houses all the records of each incarnation of anyone who has ever lived on Earth, as well as all recorded knowledge throughout humankind. The Etheric Council presides over this Hall."

"Who are they?" asked the Princess.

"The Etheric Council is made up of an advanced group of souls who have the ancient wisdom of all spiritual knowledge. They are also known as 'The Great White Brotherhood' because of their light of spirituality. Each one was picked by God for their sage wisdom as advisors." Ascending the marble steps, both girls arrived at the door to the Hall. Ainslie continued, "Here is where we part for a wee while as you have to see the Council by yourself. No need to worry, for I'll be here when you finish."

Walking into the Hall, the Princess saw the twelve-member Council seated in a semi-circle. Dressed in their long white robes with sashes of gold, they looked exactly as Ainslie had described them. The angel had explained that the 'Elders', as she lovingly referred to them, chose to look older in order to reflect the wisdom of the ages. The Etheric Council looked over their glasses at the Princess and spoke as one.

"Hello Ariel, welcome back Home. We are so pleased to see you again."

The sound of her true name, Ariel, went straight to her heart and awakened her as if out of a dream. Instantly, she recognized in her deepest knowing that this was her true name.

"Hello. I am so happy to meet with you again!"

The Etheric Council then opened a very large book on the table in front of them. This was Ariel's Book of Life and contained the information of all her incarnations and spiritual lessons. Before incarnating to Earth, all souls and the Elders wrote a sacred contract together outlining the details of that soul's upcoming incarnation. Each soul writes the contract of their life to help further their spiritual growth.

Looking over her contract, the Elders began to review Ariel's incarnation, which she had just lived as an Egyptian Princess.

"Ariel, you chose a relatively short, wealthy life of royal privilege. Explain about your experiences and the lessons that you learned."

Ariel felt very comfortable addressing the Etheric Council, as she knew in her heart that they were loving souls who only wanted the best for her.

"Firstly, I wanted to experience the love of a close-knit family. I was extremely close to my mother and I felt security and kindness from my father. I was able to experience the love of siblings with my two younger brothers and my sister.

"Secondly, I wanted to learn to assert and empower myself in that life. By contracting my marriage to a Pharaoh, I hoped to soften his heart so that he wouldn't be so cruel to his subjects." Ariel looked down and sighed deeply. "Maybe if I had denied my own selfish needs and married the Pharaoh, I could have lived a better life and gone on to soften his cruel heart, in time."

One of the Elders looked up from his thick glasses and smiled.

"Dear one, no life is better or worse than another. Remember that they are all equal in the eyes of God and your life choices were merely a teaching tool for you to grow spiritually. We have come to the conclusion that you exhibited a great deal of compassion and empowerment for one so young. You demonstrated great kindness and concern for the young handmaiden, when you could have just as easily treated her with haughty contempt. You certainly displayed your inner strength when you chose to escape from the palace. Rather than be in a loveless marriage to an old, ill Pharaoh, you dared to strive for a cherished love of your own. In fact, we applaud the choices that you made for one so young, and we see you as a very courageous and brave girl."

Surprised by their comments, Ariel beamed and she thanked them. She felt her cheeks blush and her smile reflected how proud she was of herself. Passing her Book of Life across the table, each Elder signed off on Ariel's completed contract.

Before she left, the Elders reminded her to enjoy her time at Home. "Rest, study, play and become reacquainted with loved ones. But know that in the future, you can choose whenever you want to reincarnate again to visit Earth and to grow further." Anticipating her next question, the Elders allowed Ariel to speak.

"Forgive me, but why is it encouraged to keep returning to the Earth once we have already experienced it?"

The Elders knew this was a very important question. "You see Ariel, of all the planets in all the solar systems, Earth is by far the toughest place to learn your lessons. God created our real Home of Heaven for us to be able to live in our natural state of peace, joy and bliss. Yet, because the best lessons are learned by contrast, God created Earth. You should be very proud of yourself, Ariel, as not all souls have the courage and strength to go to such a disharmonious planet and experience the challenges of duality. We are in awe of those who choose to go to Earth with all of its ego, temptation, greed, hatred and negativity. Quite frankly, we regard anyone who chooses to challenge themselves in this way to be quite a spiritual warrior."

Trying to process this information, Ariel continued, "But why does it take so long on Earth to learn our lessons when we are able to manifest things immediately here?"

"The negative energies on Earth are much denser than the light and positive energies in Heaven," the Elders replied, once again in unison. "It takes a great deal of effort to transcend these dark, heavy vibrations in order to ascend and grow spiritually. That's why ascension seems to be such a slow, laborious process as reflected in Earth-time. The main reason for incarnation is to slowly allow our lessons to be acquired thoroughly and in perfect time. After all, Ariel, the best lessons we learn are often the ones that come through hardship and adversity." The Elders smiled and nodded in agreement of their collective comment. "After all, if the lessons came easy, we wouldn't take any notice of them."

Standing and bowing, the Elders acknowledged Ariel for completing her incarnation. Proud of herself, Ariel turned and left her session with the Etheric Council. Exiting the Hall of Akashic Records, she descended the pink marble steps into a rose garden. This beautiful garden was a place to meet with loved ones after completing one's session with the Etheric Council. In this way, one could continue their homecoming celebrations. However, on this occasion, Ariel was quite alone.

Ainslie had intuited that Ariel needed time to contemplate her life as the Princess. Sitting by a nearby fountain, Ariel remembered that for every action there is a reaction. In Heaven, where everyone acts and works for the betterment of all, it was obvious that all souls were affected by the actions of other souls. But Ariel recalled that on Earth, where many people chose to be disconnected from each other, people failed to understand that what we do individually has a direct affect on all living things.

Sighing deeply, she wondered if Ainslie would return and in an instant, Ainslie appeared in front of her.

"How did you know that I was thinking about you?" said Ariel.

"It's what I do," replied Ainslie with a knowing grin. "Your guides and angels are bound to you by thought. They are so in tune with your thoughts that they hear you no matter where they are and no matter what they are doin'."

"I don't want to brag," Ainslie said, puffing out her chest, "but we often know what you're going to think before you think it. In fact, your angels are able to reply to you the same way that your thoughts come to your mind. It is not difficult to discern angelic voices from your own, as they are soft and melodic. Actually, many people say that they hear the voice of their angels not with their ears but through their hearts."

The soft tone in Ariel's voice quickly changed to one of frustration. "If you were so in tune with me, why didn't you help me when I was sad as the Princess?"

Ainslie smiled sweetly. "Ariel, my dear, your angelic assistance is never allowed to tell you what to do. God has told us that we cannot interfere with free will and free choice. If you tune in and listen, angels' soft voices can reassure and comfort you. They can only ever suggest possible options for you to choose from. But ultimately, your choices are always yours to make. But know, my dear sweet child, that your angels and guides never leave you."

Carefully thinking about Ainslie's words, Ariel then asked, "And what about all those people who met me at the end of the tunnel?

Didn't they care enough to make contact and reassure me in my sad desperation?"

"The fact that your loved ones did not speak to you doesn't mean that they don't love and care for you. Their actions are no different to other loved ones in Heaven. Many souls in Heaven know exactly what you were going through for your spiritual growth; as they have experienced similar instances in their previous incarnations. They realize that it's just a temporary state and they know what we must all go through to advance our spiritual knowledge. In addition, they knew that it would not be long before you were reunited with them once again."

A cloud suddenly came over Ariel's face. "Ainslie, why couldn't I remember you and my real Home when I was on Earth? It would have made my life so much easier."

Ainslie smiled reassuringly. "Humans must be veiled from their knowledge of Heaven in order for them to stay and complete their lessons on the Earth plane. This is called 'The Veil of Forgetfulness.' If it was not in place, life would be too much of a constant struggle as everyone would always wish to return to their blissful life in their true Home, and they simply would not choose to stay."

Strolling through the rose gardens, Ariel was feeling remarkably comfortable for having just returned from Earth. She twirled around with her hands stretched out wide. "I feel so alive and happy, yet I haven't been here for long."

Ainslie laughed and said, "You must be a very fast study. Most people take the equivalent of three Earth days to adjust and fully regain their knowledge of Heaven after they cross from the Earth plane." The reason for Ariel's quick adjustment to her real Home was obvious to Ainslie. She knew that death was a much easier event for the young and the old. An older person was often weary and ready to leave Earth, and a younger person who dies has chosen to return to Earth only for a short time and has not been as deeply invested in a long Earthly life.

Ariel stopped and listened, as she was just able to hear a faint sound of singing. "Where are those beautiful voices coming from?"

"From the Temple of Healing. Would you like to go there?"

"Very much!" Ariel replied excitedly, trying to decide which path to take. "Which way?"

"Ariel, don't you remember that a soul in Heaven can transform themselves into light and teleport to other places purely by thinkin' about it?"

"I guess some things are going to take time to get used to again," Ariel replied shyly.

"By clearin' all of our thoughts, we can focus and center our minds on the sole purpose of travelin'. In this way, all our destinations are just a thought-form away. With a little practice, this ability should return in no time at all." Ainslie stopped for a moment, deep in thought. "Come to think about it, Ariel, while this is second nature and comes easily to the souls in Heaven, one of the hardest things to re-learn on Earth is how to focus our thoughts." Shaking her head, Ainslie said, "OK, are you ready to try it?"

"Yes, I'm ready."

"Now, let's do this together," Ainslie said, taking Ariel's hand in hers. "Clear your mind of any thoughts and think travelin' and I will think about the destination."

Almost immediately, they were both standing in front of a beautiful circular building rising to a pyramidal shape made of glass with a clear quartz crystal on top. Quietly walking into the building, Ainslie whispered, "This is the Angelic Healing Temple where the souls of humans come when they are in need of comfort or healin'."

The inside of the Temple resembled a stadium with seats ascending to the top. Ainslie and Ariel silently climbed the steps.

As they climbed higher, Ainslie gestured for Ariel to look back down several stories below. A large bed covered with linens of white was positioned in the middle of the area. Surrounding the bed were crystals of every description. Ariel sat in wonder as she watched thousands of angels focusing their love and healing energies. The pyramid acted as an antenna to pick up the sounds of the prayers of those in need from the Earth plane. Ariel's heart was full of love and compassion as she listened to the sweet singing of healing prayers sung in the angelic language of light.

"What happens after a soul has had a healing" Ariel whispered.

"Humans often feel better physically or they have an awakenin' or an answer to their problem. Emotionally, they feel like they can cope better and a huge weight has been lifted off their shoulders."

Ariel's voice became choked with tears of emotion as she said, "It is truly amazing, Ainslie, just how much we are loved."

Ainslie nodded in agreement. "Ariel, for every human on Earth, there are many kindred souls in Heaven who hear our prayers. They have experienced similar situations and come to the aid of those in need. It is often when we are sleepin' that souls in Heaven send us healin' through our dream state. In this way, all dreams hold important information for the recipient, for they are all connected to God." Ainslie paused for a moment before continuing. "Would you like to see the levels where you will be studyin' and workin'?"

"I thought Heaven was supposed to be fun and we didn't have to do any work here."

"Well, maybe the word 'work' doesn't best describe pursuin' what we are passionate about. In Heaven, we only do those things that make us happy. Come with me; it will become clearer when you see the different levels."

As they walked out of the Angelic Healing Temple, Ainslie explained, "You see, Ariel, Heaven is divided into various levels in which souls can live and work in different groups, dependin' on their interests and passions. It is much like Earth, where people of similar consciousness, purposes, and areas of study gravitate towards one another. In this way, they have common interests and feel more comfortable and supported in their surroundings."

Eagerly listening, Ariel said, "Now I understand. I have already been to two of those levels."

Ainslie nodded her head in agreement, "That's right; the first was the transition level where you were reacquainted with your loved ones. Although it is only a transitory level, it is a significant area for those souls returnin' to Heaven and those leavin' Heaven. Many souls who have denied their Divine nature and are not consciously aware of Heaven can have an awful shock here. This area helps people adjust before goin' on to the next level."

"And the second level I experienced was the re-orientation level," Ariel offered, "where I reviewed my life, met with the Etheric Council to remember my contract, and became re-educated to regain my powers."

"You do catch on fast. But now the fun part really starts. Ariel, I want you to close your eyes and think about animals."

Although she was confused by this strange request, Ariel closed her eyes and immediately found herself on a new level. This was the level where all animals resided, as well as those who had a love for gardening. This extraordinary level gave nature lovers endless opportunities to cultivate in this true gardener's paradise. And best of all, there were no insects.

Walking through the vividly colored flowers, Ariel was marveling at the enormous plants. Everywhere she looked, people were digging in the soil and nurturing the beauty and bounties of nature. Ariel let out a gasp; as she couldn't believe her eyes. Wandering out of the forest and strolling in front of her was a lion and a lamb.

Noticing Ariel's amazed expression, Ainslie said, "It does seem very odd but both wild and domesticated animals live side by side in complete harmony. This is because they simply do not hunt. Animal lovers on this level are truly in Heaven as they can fully communicate with their furry friends. This area holds all the pets that cross over as well and is quite a favorite; even with those who work on different levels." Ainslie bent down to pat the lion and scratch its neck. "Oh I do love this level. Come on, Ariel, there's more to see. But remember when we get there, be careful where you step."

In a blink of an eye, easels, paints and pottery wheels surrounded Ariel and Ainslie. This huge studio saw many renowned artists throughout history creating side by side. Ariel said, "Where are we now?"

"Keep movin' or someone will try to paint or sculpt you. This is the artistic level and it is broken up into sections. In this area are the writers, painters, sculptors, and crafts people and ..." In the flash of a thought, both girls were standing in another section and Ainslie continued without missing a beat, "... this wonderful section includes the entire world's music from the composers, singers, musicians and entertainers. This is an amazing creative level as there are also people who are artistic in their careers like architecture, cooking, fashion and interior design, just to name a few areas."

"Being around these creative people would be so inspirational and I could learn so much."

Ainslie laughed, "And they could learn so much from you as well. It sounds like you've already made up your mind to stay here."

"Maybe so, but I will wait until I have seen all the other levels."

With that, Ainslie showed Ariel the fifth level of Heaven. Ainslie explained that this level was for all the scientific and technological researchers and laboratories researching everything from the cures for diseases to new advances in technology.

"What I like best about this level," said Ainslie, "is that everyone is workin' for the betterment of all. Nobody has to work in secret or hide their research; as there is no jealousy, competition or fear of discovery here. Everyone benefits from each other's work and findings."

Ainslie glanced over to her friend. "Ariel, there is another interesting section of this level. It is for those souls who take on the mission of spreadin' God's love. Sometimes referred to as Walk-ins, they come back to Earth to wake people up to their Divine nature. They help them remember that they are love and that we are all one. Unlike other souls who have been veiled with the forgetfulness of Heaven, Walk-ins are spiritually advanced beings who return to Earth fully awakened as messengers of God's love. In this way, they help others open up to a greater understandin' of their own spirituality. Once you sign on for such a mission, you basically give your life to God and, in many ways, your life is not your own. Doin' everything to spread God's love, Walk-ins will often find themselves involved in many areas to share their spiritual knowledge, speakin' openly about Heaven. These beautiful souls are very different from others and can be identified by the radiance or light that is shining from them."

"It sounds as if it would be a very difficult life."

"For some souls, there is no greater mission on Earth than to be in God's service. By tellin' others about non-judgment, forgiveness and acceptance, Walk-ins hope that the world will one day live in unity and unconditional love for all. Their service is to spread God's word of livin' in harmony and peace."

Ariel felt a lump in her throat. "They sound like very special people."

"In God's eyes, we are all special people," Ainslie gently replied. "Now there, Missy, are you ready for the sixth level?" Instantly, both girls were facing a large blackboard and the chalk dust made Ariel sneeze. Glancing around at a classroom, she asked, "Where are we now Ainslie?"

"Ariel, this is the sixth level where lecturers, counselors and teachers reside. One may choose to become proficient in any subject studied here. There are endless libraries and research centers. The counselors on this level help children who are enterin' or leavin' Heaven and also work with those souls who are suffering from trauma. This level is also of great importance because souls are taught how to be spirit guides. In fact, almost everyone will have the chance to be a spirit guide at some time. This is somewhat of a payback system, since at one time or another someone was a spirit guide to you."

In wonderment, Ariel gazed at Ainslie. "What could possibly be left after all of this?"

"Well, there is one more level left, but I am only allowed to explain it to you, as we are unable to visit there."

Ariel was intrigued. "Why is that?"

"The seventh level is for those who want to return their energies back to God Source itself. People ask to give up their individuality and let their vibrations get reabsorbed in the 'All That Is,' or the one Divine

Source. Those souls who have lived an exceptionally devotional life may choose this, but it is a very rare occurrence."

Shaking her head in amazement, Ariel said, "Ainslie, if Heaven is such a beautiful place, why are people so scared of crossing over?"

Ainslie smiled. "People are only afraid of death if they have allowed themselves to become disconnected from God's love. In truth, we are all one and come from the same God Source, and we can never be disconnected from God's love. In fact, the transition between life and what so many people call death needn't be so great. Throughout history, there have lived spiritually advanced souls on Earth who create and live a 'Heaven on Earth' existence. Once souls understand that their physical death is not the end of their existence, they don't seem to be upset by it occurring. They consciously live their life, but know when they cross over that they will be goin' to their one true Home."

"But why would a person choose not to feel God's beautiful love?"

"God has given us free will and free choice, Ariel. We can choose to think that we are unloved by God or even that He does not exist. In this way, many people constantly deny their Divine connection and choose to live very unhappy, negative lives."

Ainslie read Ariel's thoughts and she could sense that she was holding back another question. "You are wonderin' in all the levels I showed you, why I haven't mentioned anything about those people who deliberately hurt others."

"Yes, well, I was thinking about those who choose to be apart from God. What happens to those who live a life of cruelty towards others? It was very obvious in the life I just lived where class distinction meant that royalty had the right to mistreat and dispose of others at will."

"Yes, Ariel, for those souls there are the dark planes of Heaven. These planes house souls who deliberately hurt another for their gain or benefit. When a person finds themselves on this plane, they notice the energies are very dense and heavy. Yet unlike the fiery flames of Hell that are so often depicted in many Earth books and religions, God does not want anyone to unnecessarily suffer.

"The surroundings on this dark plane are simple, not beautiful and welcomin' like other levels of Heaven. They have to meet with God and the Etheric Council to review their lives and re-live every thought and feelin' of their victims. They must be made to experience how one's destructive actions affects another. The only way to get out of the darker planes of Heaven is by choosin' to return to Earth to experience another incarnation, but this time choosin' a life which is more in alignment with God's love. By bein' on the receivin' end of cruelty, they have the opportunity to be held accountable for their actions. In this way, experience often becomes our best teacher in order for us to be able to advance spiritually. "

Deep in thought for a moment, Ariel then said, "Surely, Ainslie, when we take on the human form, I'm thinking that everyone in their life has told a lie, or mistreated or mislead someone. Shouldn't we all be on the dark plane?"

The angel laughed. "Wow, maybe you should live and work with the philosophers. No, my dear. If one is on this dense level, it signifies that most of their lifetime was spent treatin' others with cruelty and makin' certain that others around them felt smaller and insignificant and made others fear them.

"It's strange on Earth that the worst crime one can commit is to murder another. But the worst crime in God's mind is the systematic emotional torture and torment of a person's soul. These beautiful souls start to lose their inner light and they need much more time to recover from their horrendous experiences. To hurt one knowingly by emotional torture is one of the cruelest things one can do to another on the Earth."

Ariel was physically affected by Ainslie's explanation. "My heart weighs heavy for all those people who have had their souls emotionally tortured."

"I can feel the compassion and the tender understandin' in your heart, Ariel. You demonstrated this when you showed kindness to the poor handmaiden who attended you as a Princess. And remember, just because you contracted for your own power to be taken away through a forced marriage, you chose not to cave in but defiantly kept your own inner light by trying to escape."

Although Ainslie had spoken of many things, none of it was new to Ariel. With each bit of information that was 'reintroduced,' she was able to vividly remember her life in Heaven. Bursting into a huge smile, Ariel said in an excited tone, "I now get to choose, don't I?"

"Aye, you do," Ainslie laughed. "You now get to choose your house. So, Ariel, where are you going to live?"

3

Heaven – Manifesting Your Dream Home

The words had barely left Ainslie's lips when Ariel focused her attention on the mental images of her house, and immediately it began to manifest. Appearing in front of her were open fields completely covered with sunflowers. The rows of cypress trees cast long shadows across the hillside, and the intensity and clarity of the light could only have been in one place.

Giggling and rubbing her stomach, Ainslie said, "Hmmm, I am gettin' a cravin' for pizza."

Ariel smiled. "That's right, hold the anchovies."

In that instant, her Italian villa started to appear. The sunflowers on the adjacent fields turned their heads to Ariel as if to welcome her home. Similar to an eager painter who impatiently splashes paint on a canvas, her excited thoughts rapidly brought more of her house into view. As the details of her villa and the surrounding beauty of the Tuscan hills became more clearly defined, familiar images started to materialize. Her vegetable garden brought forth blood-red vine-ripened tomatoes, dark green cucumbers, lettuce and *melanzane*. Oops! She meant to say 'eggplant' but she felt so comfortable in her surroundings that the Italian language was quickly coming back.

As she walked up the path to her villa, she turned to see the dark purple grapes on the vines climbing the nearby hills. Facing her villa once again, a pergola appeared next to the house and was instantly draped with perfumed jasmine and red and purple bougainvillea. Following the path around the side of the house, Ariel watched as a hand-painted tiled outdoor area sprung up under her feet. Huge mosaic urns filled with brightly colored cyclamens, bluebells, violets and geraniums placed themselves along the carved balustrade hugging the outdoor area. Walking over to its railing, Ariel gazed over the side and saw a dramatic drop onto an expansive, lush valley leading to snowcapped mountains in the distance.

The sun lounge underneath the large shade umbrella looked so inviting that she lay down and closed her eyes. Her reverie didn't last long, however, as the air was suddenly filled with barking.

"*Dio mio! Ciao*, Cleo," Ariel squealed. A teeny, chestnut brown Yorkshire terrier skidded across the tiles and leapt into Ariel's arms. Snuggling her nose in Cleo's fur, Ariel's heart was overjoyed at being reunited with her little friend once more.

As the last rays of sun struggled to shine, Ariel watched as dusk fell over her valley. Entering the arched doorway of her villa, with its weathered antique wooden doors, her eyes locked on to the large red leather sofa strewn with soft embroidered pillows. The color of the couch reflected the same color of the burnt red soil. The open fireplace reminded her of those times that she had chosen to feel the cold and snuggle under the warmth of a cashmere blanket.

Looking over the open plan area into the large, well-appointed kitchen, the hanging metal pots seemed to wink, encouraging her to prepare a feast. Her kitchen had seen many delicious meals prepared for cherished friends. And although one didn't have to eat to be nourished in Heaven, the joy of preparing beautiful meals and sampling wonderful cuisine could still be experienced. Walking into her bedroom, her four-poster canopy bed was immediately draped in pure white damask material. The bed was facing a huge picture window looking out at the stars that began to shimmer in the sky.

Passing by the full-length mirror, Ariel saw a very different image to that of the Princess. Her girlish body now sported womanly curves and her traditional black, angular, Egyptian hairstyle had been replaced by long, soft blonde curls. Opening her wardrobe, there appeared lovely flowing dresses and many pairs of silver slippers. Smiling to herself, she had no idea where her love of silver sandals had come from; all she knew was that they made her happy.

Putting on a lavender gown and choosing a pair of slippers, Ariel went to the lounge room and sat by the comfortable bay window overlooking the fields. The moon had risen and was casting a silvery light on the sleeping sunflowers. As she closed her eyes, Cleo jumped up and nestled deep in her lap. Ariel whispered softly, "Thank you, Ainslie, thank you, God, thank you for my one true Home."

As there is no time in Heaven, it's difficult to tell how long Ariel chose to rest at her beautiful villa. Days were filled with walking the undulating hills and getting reacquainted with the locals. Her daily ritual was to hop on her bicycle, put tiny Cleo into the basket and ride into the nearby village. She would fill an entire morning enjoying a coffee, speaking to her friends, selecting some interesting 'essentials' at the delicatessen, as well as picking up freshly baked bread. Enjoying the panoply of her quaint little village, life was unhurried with a gentle rhythm all its own.

Today, unlike other days, she decided it was not a day for bike riding. Nestled under a blanket, sitting in her bay window, she chose to read and look out on a rainy day. Cleo cuddled into her lap and was happy to snuggle deep into the covers. Though Ariel could have chosen any weather, there was something comforting about being inside and protected on a wet day. Softly she giggled to herself. Fully conscious that she was in Heaven, how much more protected could she be?!

Watching the rain drip off the flowers that were hanging from the pergola, she felt an urge to play the piano. It had been a long time since she had thought about her beloved instrument. Turning to Cleo, she said, "You know, I think I'm ready to play again." Just then Ariel sensed that someone was walking up the path. Opening the front door, she saw a dark, handsome man about to knock.

"I felt that you wanted to make beautiful music together once again," he said.

A huge smile beamed across Ariel's face as she threw her arms around her beloved Twin Flame. "Your timing, Kiel, as always, is divine."

Kissing her sweetly, Kiel smiled at Ariel. "It doesn't come as a surprise when two people are so in sync with one another." Holding out his hand to her, he said, "Shall we?"

"I can't think of anything I would rather do," said Ariel, accepting his invitation.

Immediately, Kiel and Ariel found themselves on the fourth level of Heaven. Passionate musicians welcomed them as they channeled the inspiration of God. The genre of music didn't matter, nor the era it came from; these gifted musicians shared a burning desire in their hearts to create music. No matter how many times Ariel returned, she was never quite ready for the overwhelming sense of joy she felt when playing music.

Setting forth to find her piano, Ariel said to Kiel, "I still find it amazing that every time Earth needs to be uplifted, one of these creative geniuses goes back to infuse the planet with more light."

Nodding his head, Kiel replied, "That's right, Ariel, but not just in the area of music. Gifted painters, poets and writers have all contributed to the wealth of extraordinary works on the Earth plane. The works of art that are fashioned here bring increased joy and knowledge to a world that is thirsting for beauty."

She suddenly stopped walking, as there in front of her was her lifelong friend. The gleam from her beautiful baby grand piano enticed her to come and play. Sitting down on the leather-tooled bench, her hands gently rested on the keys. Ariel was like all the others on this level; they were fashioned by God to feel 'alive' through inspired, artistic creation.

She thought back to the talented musicians who had played for her family in her life of privilege as a Princess. It was so obvious from their expressions that their inspired playing was coming from another place; that other place was Heaven.

As she began to play, the other musicians sensed her joy and applauded as the music flowed from her once again. The hours passed like minutes and it was soon time to return to her beloved villa.

Gazing over her grape arbor, she watched as the last grapes were being harvested and taken to be crushed into wine. She thought how nice it would be to host a meal to go along with the wine from her valley. Excited by this thought, she walked into her kitchen, grabbed her apron from behind the door and started to prepare a celebration feast, while mentally gathering all her friends.

In her present reality, all she had to do was to think about what she wanted to serve and it would manifest immediately. Yet, cooking was similar to her talents in music and she loved the creative process. Standing in front of her huge wooden table, she mentally ticked off all the ingredients for the feast.

Taking the bright red tomatoes, fresh garlic, and basil from her garden, she began to mix the ingredients for a delicious sauce. Setting it on the big stove, she then decided to make fresh pasta. Liberally dusting the counter with flour, she added water and a little oil and started to knead and roll the dough. She was startled by a sudden sneeze from under the counter. Cleo was now sporting a white nose as a result of the flying flour. Assessing the dough, Ariel decided that today she would be making gnocchi and she set about carefully rolling and imprinting each one with a fork. With the gnocchi and the sauce completed, Ariel proceeded to make her famous eggplant parmagiana and a large salad brimming with fresh vegetables.

Wiping her hands on her apron, she walked under the pergola and gazed at the table. Just thinking about the upcoming feast, the table had set itself with antique china that had an exquisite Etruscan hand-painted pattern.

Breaking up the crusty, fresh bread into bite-sized pieces, Ariel placed them in the silver bread bowl. The day was warm but not too hot and the beauty of the sun-kissed hills seemed even more breathtaking.

"Hello. Something sure smells good." A soft, familiar voice preceded a lady with short black hair, luminous white skin, sapphire blue eyes and freckles. Shania had been one of her spirit guides in a former incarnation and had provided Ariel with much-needed help and comfort. Embracing each other, they looked out the window and saw Kiel leading a large group of people. It was wonderful to sit down and chat with old friends. (Funny how she thought to call them 'old friends' when many in Heaven chose to appear to be around twenty-five to thirty-five years of age.) The afternoon was spent reminiscing with cherished loved ones about times shared and recalling different past lives together.

After a sumptuous feast and a beautiful day, Ariel and Kiel waved goodbye to the last of the guests. They prepared one last espresso and went out on the moonlit patio to gaze at the stars. Wrapped in Kiel's arms, Ariel sighed at the thought of how much she had missed beautiful days just like this one.

Cleo began to bark and became very excited. Ariel slowly put down her cup. "Yes, little one, I sensed that she was approaching as well." Moving towards the door, Ariel opened it to find Ainslie standing in front of her.

"Hello, Ariel, it's lovely to see you again. You certainly have settled back beautifully. But I bring you a message from the Elders. They would like to speak with you."

It dawned on Ariel why it had been so important for her to gather all her friends and see them once again. In fact, for several days she had been sensing deep in her heart that something would be taking her away from her beautiful villa. She had been enjoying herself so much that she kept postponing answering their call. Turning to Kiel, they embraced tenderly. Although they missed each other when they were apart, they knew that an Earth life was equivalent to only a few weeks in Heaven's time.

Ariel picked up Cleo, kissed her head and handed the little ball of fur to Kiel.

"Would you see that she gets to the third level so that she can be looked after while I'm away?"

"I would love to."

Ariel then said her goodbyes to her beautiful villa. And in a blink of an eye, she found herself in front of the Hall of the Akashic Records.

No matter how many times Ariel stood in front of this magnificent pink marble building, she was overwhelmed by its majesty and hanging gardens. As she walked up the steps, she felt the spray from the cascading waterfalls off the surrounding mountains. Breathing deeply, she enjoyed the scent of the beautiful displays of flowers. Entering the golden doors, she walked into the hall where the familiar semi-circle of the Etheric Council was seated. Out of respect, she stood quietly and waited for the Elders to address her.

"Hello again, dear Ariel. We are very happy that you have been enjoying yourself back Home. The music that you have been composing is so soothing. Have you been channeling it down to Earth through any spirit guides?"

Upon hearing the Elders' high praise for her music, Ariel smiled. "Yes, my wonderful friend Shania is a spirit guide to a talented young man on Earth. She has met with his soul during his dream state and presented him with some of my music. Through his intuition, he has been inspired to remember and write down the lovely melodies."

"Ariel, your music contains more than just pleasant sounds. When souls hear those tones, which contain deep love and compassion, the sound awakens them to their true, Divine nature. We thank you for your contribution that you have made to many."

"Happy to be of service, though I feel that was not the only reason you called me here today." Even though Ariel's intuition had anticipated this meeting for awhile, she always felt a rush in her heart and a nervous excitement in her stomach when she was asked to meet with the Elders. Opening up her Book of Life, the wise sages found her last life experience on Earth.

"The life you chose as a Princess in Egypt was both privileged and short. The hardship you endured was in the last month of your life. Last time you were with us, we spoke about the lessons that you had learned from your experience." Silently reading over her contract, one of the Elders cleared his throat. "Ariel, did you realize what effect your actions had on others in that lifetime?"

"I really didn't think about it."

"Did you realize that your treatment of the handmaiden Maat had a wonderful effect on the other slaves? Maat had spoken to them of your kindness towards her. You never knew it, but in that one small act of compassion, you gave them hope that those in royal positions might also see them as human beings and not just servants. It's very important to realize that what we do on Earth is meant not only for us to ascend and grow, but each one of us is a walking example to others on how to act in a loving, compassionate and kind manner. That is why everything we do truly does have an impact on everyone else."

Looking over his thick glasses, another one of the Elders continued, "There is a dire need for more light to be brought to a tiny village in Scotland that is weighed down by constant tyranny and hopeless conditions. Hope, dear Ariel, is sometimes the only thing a person needs in order to rekindle the Divine spark of God within. You showed enormous strength of character and conviction in your last incarnation. Would you be willing to help and be the light that lifts hope in this depressed village?"

A big smile spread across Ariel's face. "Perhaps this was the reason I chose a Scottish angel in Ainslie to accompany me on my journey back Home."

Smiling knowingly, the Elders said in unison, "Well there are no coincidences."

"Actually, I can't wait to go back. I have been thinking for a while of what I want to write into my new contract."

"We sensed as much, Ariel." The Council smiled. "We love your enthusiasm. Tell us what you want to experience in your new life."

Taking time to consider her contract, Ariel responded, "I know in my heart that the only way to grow spiritually is to be tested. I would really like to challenge myself in my next life." With the location and era having already been determined by the Elders, Ariel then carefully chose the lessons she wanted to learn. To aid her, she also chose her family, their characteristics and the events of her life that would challenge and strengthen her spiritual growth.

Presenting the new contract in her Book of Life, the Etheric Council read it aloud to Ariel. Agreeing to experience this new life, Ariel put her signature on the contract. Thanking the Elders, she left the Hall of Akashic Records and focused her thoughts on the transition level. Instantly, she appeared on the same level that she had stepped onto after exiting the tunnel and arriving in Heaven.

Looking around the platform, she saw many souls waiting to re-enter Earth's physical dimension. Yet, unlike the bewildered expressions of those people who re-enter Heaven, these people knew full well about their pre-written contracts and where they were going. Waiting to be called, Ariel's thoughts turned to her beloved Kiel. She sighed, as she would miss him terribly. Yet, she reminded herself that a normal lifespan on the Earth plane was a mere few weeks in Heaven's time.

Hearing her name, she walked over to the platform near the outgoing tunnel. Mentally passing on a thought of love and kisses to her beloved dog Cleo, she told her telepathically that she would be back soon.

In that instant, Ariel stepped into the tunnel and a great whooshing sound was heard.

4

Berwick, Scotland, 1344

The whooshing noise of the tunnel was immediately drowned out by a huge, guttural scream, followed by grunting and panting noises. Waiting for the next unbearable wave of contraction pains to crash upon her, Margret Mary MacDonald stopped her field work, ran to a thicket of roses by the edge of the field, and lifted her skirts.

Squatting down over a patch of grass, she screamed as the baby's head crowned. In the momentary wait between contractions, Margret Mary braced herself against a tree and prayed for just one more push. As the next blast of excruciating pain hit, Margret Mary pushed with all her might. And plop, the baby dropped in the grass beneath her skirts. Margret Mary removed her dirty pinafore and wiped off the baby. Picking up her scythe, she cut the umbilical cord. Looking at the bright red flowers on a nearby rosebush and her daughter's fiery red hair, she said, "Aye, that's what I'll call you, Annabel Rose."

She proceeded to unbutton the top of her dress, put the babe to her breast and swaddled and secured the infant tightly to her chest. Buttoning up her dress, Margret Mary went back to harvesting the wheat.

Getting back in line with all the others, she started once again to rhythmically sway and swing her scythe. The rays of the late afternoon sun softly disappeared behind the hilltop. This meant one blessed thing; it was time to go home.

Walking from the field, Margret Mary peeked into her dress and took the first long glance at child number ten. Unlike her other brown-eyed children, this baby had bright, cornflower blue eyes that seemed to convey a deep knowing to Margret Mary's soul. As chills ran up and down her spine, she felt her body shiver as a sign of confirmation. In that instant, she knew that this child shared her gift of prophecy.

Her elation immediately turned to dread as it dawned on her that her husband would curse and beat her for producing another girl. Men needed strong, robust sons, not daughters, to help them work the land. Girls were useless and a burden to feed and to look after. It was customary for all girls of very little means to be married off at an early age. A young, strong bride often meant a good and prodigious breeder. Margret Mary's mother was fourteen when she gave birth to her. And at age fifteen, Margret Mary had been married off to a man of thirty years. Almost every year since then, she had given birth. Yet with the squalid, harsh conditions in which they lived, the infant mortality rate was enormous. For this reason, only five of Margret Mary's ten children had survived.

Bellowing at the top of her lungs, she called for her other children, "Kyle, Bonnie, Fiona, Jean." Their four heads popped up through the long grass where they had been playing. Dutifully, they ran over to her. With her son and three daughters trailing behind her, Margret Mary wearily set off on the long path that would take them home.

Although utterly exhausted after giving birth and working the Baron's land, Margret Mary drew in a deep breath, exhaled and forced herself to keep going. In the 1300s, a high-ranking Baron or Lord owned the land on which a serf lived. In exchange for the right to live on and work the land, the Baron enforced high taxes on the goods produced. This often meant that the family barely had enough to survive.

In addition, whatever meager amount was left over, families were ordered to tithe to the Church. There were many instances of Church collectors visiting families who pleaded that they didn't have anything more to give. It was amazing that after burning and maiming family members before their eyes, how quickly someone remembered coins or some jewels that had been buried deep beneath the Earth. It was common knowledge that if one did not tithe to the Church, your family would be condemned as sinners, damned and forced to burn in hell for all eternity.

To this never-ending cycle of abject poverty and servitude was added your obligation to the Church. One day a week, you were forced to work Church land. The Church kept those goods that were produced because this was seen as your religious duty.

It had been an unusual few days, as all serfs living on the Baron's land were relieved of their normal work and summoned to bring in the harvest. Working the serfs from sunrise to sunset for three solid days made great economic sense. The fact that they were pulled away from working the Baron's land, which diminished the production of their own goods, was of no concern to the Baron. There would be no concessions on the taxes, which they would later have to pay. The serfs would somehow have to work harder and make up for their lost time.

Watching the fading afternoon light, Margret Mary growled at her children to quicken their steps. Maybe this was more of a reminder to herself that wolves roamed these forests and that it was in everyone's best interest to be indoors by dark. Suddenly, the silent newborn whimpered and became agitated, as if she were very frightened.

Instantly, Margret Mary's intuition told her to get off the path and hide her family in the deep thicket. Scurrying under scrub and hidden by the dark green foliage, Margret Mary pushed her children's heads down into the dark soil. A cloud of dust appeared in the distance and a band of riders thundered towards them. It was not uncommon for thieves to set off into the forests at dusk to steal, murder and rape. The family lay frozen, completely still for a long time after the riders had passed. Opening her dress, Margret Mary peeked in and kissed the now silent Annabel Rose. She mentally thanked her newborn for warning them of the danger.

As they resumed their walk home, Margret Mary was relieved

as they turned a bend in the road and she saw their thatched roof in the distance.

Walking into their hut, Margret Mary opened her blouse, unwrapped her soiled newborn and grabbed some material. No more than two hours old, Annabel Rose already had her fair share of lice from her mother. Drawing water from the large kettle over the hearth, Margret Mary wiped off Annabel Rose and swaddled her tightly. Kissing her on the forehead, she then placed her on a wooden palette of hay.

Calling to her four-year-old, Margret Mary said, "Jean, look after your sister. I've got to bring in the animals. Kyle, go and collect the chickens."

Leading the cow, the goat and the pigs through the entrance of the hut, Margret Mary stored the animals in a fenced-off area inside the house. If they were left outside, either the wild animals would make a meal out of them or the black cover of night would veil marauding thieves who could strip a village of all its livestock in no time.

Once the animals had been secured, Margret Mary saw to dinner. Swinging the large iron arm out of the fireplace, she took the lid off a huge pot. As not much stew was left, she took some black bread, goat cheese and peas and beans to supplement the meal.

After her family had quickly finished their meager meal, the three girls snuggled together on a bed of straw and fell asleep. Checking the latch on the door, Margret Mary lay down next to her newborn and started to feed her. She tried to thank the Lord for all His infinite blessings, but within seconds she was fast asleep.

Such was the life into which Annabel Rose MacDonald chose to be born.

She also chose to be a part of a village of forty families living and working on the Baron's land. These families provided the services of tradespeople, who allowed a bartering system of survival. In addition, her fellow villagers provided protection from villains and thieves.

Life in such a village often meant that you lived and died never having ventured more than a few miles from your birthplace. The furthest that most villagers traveled was to the Baron's castle, where her father had journeyed over a week ago. The castle was a day's journey by foot. The Baron had summoned men in the village to attend to repairs around his estate. Margret Mary's husband, Angus would return when the work was completed.

The next morning, Margret Mary arose while it was still dark, fed the livestock and prepared a stew to simmer throughout the day. By the time she finished cooking and baking, the sun was already high in the sky as she set off to weed the vegetable garden. She strapped little Annabel Rose inside her dress and picked up a large basket.

Opening the gate to the garden, Margret Mary noticed that the lettuce tops had been carefully nibbled away. "Bleedin' rabbits," she said out loud. Putting down her basket and bending over to pull the weeds, she made a mental note to find the hole in the fence where the rabbits were getting in.

Two large arms wrapping around her waist suddenly startled her. Letting out a scream, she fought to escape. A familiar voice bellowed, "You're not as round as you were when I left ye. Feels like you have a surprise for me." Turning around, Margret Mary looked up into her husband's face. Slowly she unbuttoned her dress and Annabel Rose's blue eyes peeked out. Picking up the baby, Angus announced, "He'll be called Lachlan, after me own Da."

Margret Mary started to tremble. In a hesitant, shaky voice she said, "I'm sorry, Angus, but her name is Annabel Rose. It's another girl."

The elated expression on Angus's face suddenly turned dark. Thrusting the baby back into Margret Mary's arms, he slapped his wife across the face. "Can't ye do anything right, damn woman? Am I to be the laughing stock of the whole village?" Enraged, he stormed off.

Fighting back the tears, Margret Mary re-swaddled Annabel Rose and continued her work in the garden. As tears tumbled down her cheeks and soaked the freshly pulled weeds, she dreamed of escaping her harsh life.

As Annabel Rose grew older, Margret Mary noted her daughter's strong love of the Earth. Perhaps it was because she was born directly onto the ground that Annabel Rose shared her mother's deep affinity with nature. The little girl would sit for hours as her mother taught her about flowers and trees. With her heightened sense of observation, she was able to easily retain the knowledge of the medicinal uses of plants and herbs.

It was uncanny how attuned Annabel Rose was to the rhythms of Mother Nature. She knew how and when to plant depending on the waxing and waning of the moon. Her keen intuitive nature helped her listen to the birds' songs and interpret their messages. She particularly loved searching and digging for crystals. Proudly bringing home the treasures that she found, her mother would then school her in their healing properties.

Although Margret Mary taught all her girls to weave, sew, cook and bake, unlike her sisters, Annabel Rose showed absolutely no interest in these activities. She would squirm and fidget until she was allowed to run outside and down to the stream. Sitting silently as she watched the water trip over rocks and stones, the rhythmic flowing spoke to the beating of her heart. Surrounded by nature, she felt contentment once again. Foraging until the last sliver of light left the sky, she would return home laden down with berries, crystals and herbs to mix up for elixirs. With the passing years, it became more and more obvious to Margret Mary that Annabel Rose's gift of prophecy was so much stronger than her own.

As a woman, Margret Mary knew how dangerous it was to be seen to know 'too much.' For that reason she had always underplayed her psychic abilities and kept her own powers a secret. She had hoped that she could do the same for her daughter. Yet, this was not to be.

Every Sunday, all the villagers were expected to attend church. Rather than a loving experience to help encourage and support another soul, church attendance was more a reminder of control and exertion of power. Living in a small village meant that everyone knew everything about each other's lives. The social pressure to conform and not appear different was stifling.

Waking early, Margret Mary forced her exhausted body to rise in order to prepare her family to attend church. The last several years had seemed much harsher, as her husband's violent outbursts had gotten worse. As she dutifully readied the children for church, she fought back tears as she recalled being forced to go to a church wedding many years ago. Angus had married off their beautiful and beloved daughter at the tender age of twelve. Margret Mary pleaded with her husband that she was far too young to be married. Yet, a gentleman of some means was traveling through the village and showed an interest in the young girl. Angus wanted to finally be rid of his obligation and burden to feed another mouth.

Margret Mary remembered running after the cart and tearfully waving goodbye to her beautiful daughter. The man lived in a township in the coastal far north and she knew in her heart that she would never see her precious daughter again.

Organizing her children into the wagon, she sighed as she looked at the empty seats and reflected on the children that she had lost to illness. Margret Mary's heart broke with the reminder of having buried four of her babies who had contracted fever and had not lived past their third birthdays. Heaving a huge sigh, she picked up the reins and yelled, "Angus, if you don't come now, we will all be late."

Bursting out the door, one arm in his woolen shirt, he yelled, "Shut up, woman, lest ye want to feel the back of me hand again!" Grabbing the reins from her, they made their way to church in silence.

The church was a massive stone building with its steeple rising high into the sky. Its towering size allowed others from far and wide to always be aware that God was watching them. And its thick, impenetrable stonewalls provided a safe fortress if the village ever fell under siege.

Sitting in the pews waiting for the service to begin, Annabel Rose was seated next to her mother. Now in her twelfth year, her long, red hair had grown brighter and seemed to reflect her outspoken, fiery nature. A young woman and a little girl with long brown hair slid along the pew until she was sitting next to Annabel Rose. "Hello, Cait!"

"Hello, Annabel Rose."

Annabel Rose tilted her head and took a long look at Cait's mother. Without any hesitation, she spoke aloud, "Cait, you must be happy that after three brothers, your mother is finally going to give you a sister."

Suddenly, the congregation went deathly quiet. Cait's mother gasped in horror. She grabbed Cait's hand and ran out of the church. Annabel Rose looked around to see the parishioners staring at her.

As was the custom, the priest commenced the service in Latin. Having neither comprehension nor understanding of Latin, the serfs stared in awe at the Priest as he spoke in what many considered to be the language of magic.

After the service had finished, everyone congregated on the church grounds to socialize and catch up on gossip. As soon as Annabel Rose came out with Margret Mary, Cait's mother burst through the crowd and ran over to Annabel Rose and grabbed her. Twisting her arm violently, she screamed, "You spying little bitch. How do you know about the baby? Nobody knows. Who told you?"

Annabel Rose looked kindly at the lady and said, "Ma'am, beggin' your pardon, nobody told me. I can see it in yer belly."

Spitting at Annabel Rose, Cait's mother's angry words flew from her lips. "You little witch, you're lying. I'll beat it out of you!"

As she raised her hand, Margret Mary stepped between them and defended her daughter. "Leave her alone. It is your own shame and embarrassment that stings, not my daughter's comments." Quickly pushing Annabel Rose along to their cart, Margret Mary could feel the burning eyes of the villagers on her neck. She knew that this was only the beginning.

"Why was Cait's mother so upset?" Annabel Rose questioned in a calm voice. "It was a beautiful bonny girl I did see." Margret Mary did not know what to tell her daughter. Cait's father had deserted his family a year ago and fled to the city. This being the case, she must have slept with a man out of wedlock. This was a sin of whoring and would be met with public punishment and shame. Hiding behind the cart with Annabel Rose, Margret Mary waited for Angus and her children to join them, trying to ignore the gathering and stares from the parishioners. She knew that those gatherings would produce seeds of gossip that would not only grow and cast a shadow on her daughter's gifts, but would be the cause of great concern for Margret Mary over the safety of her daughter.

The following morning, while Margret Mary and Annabel Rose were tending the vegetable garden, they heard a voice calling to them. Looking up, Margret Mary saw her friend Heather walking towards them, accompanied by her lame daughter, Ainslie.

"Good morrow to you, Margret Mary. I would like to have a word with young Annabel Rose." Ainslie put down her cane and sat in the grass.

Furrowing her brow, Margret Mary said, "What do you want with my Annabel Rose?" Reaching into her apron, Heather took out a small leather purse. Opening it, she handed Annabel Rose a silver coin. With tears in her eyes, Heather said, "Me poor Ainslie has been lame since birth and I would give anything for her to walk freely. No man will marry her like this and without a husband she will be shamed for all her days. I saw what happened yesterday at church with Annabel Rose. Could she please help us?"

Laying Ainslie down on the grass, Annabel Rose placed her hands around the girl's leg. She breathed deeply and felt a rush of God's healing light go through her and into Ainslie's body. Tilting her head upwards, as if connecting with Divine inspiration, Annabel Rose spoke in a deep voice not her own, "Make a poultice of fennel, sage and comfrey and bandage the leg twice a day and it will strengthen over time."

Standing up, Ainslie began to walk freely, unaided by her cane. Astonished, both mother and daughter began to cry. Through tears of joy, Ainslie's mother said, "You are indeed blessed by God, Annabel Rose." She took out her coin purse, upturned it and emptied the entire contents into Annabel Rose's hand. "How can we ever thank ye? God has blessed you with a wonderful gift, child."

In this way, Annabel Rose MacDonald started her life as a healer.

From that day forth, her life became very different. Setting up a small hut apart from her parent's house, she started to help heal others. Once the villagers experienced her healing gifts, people came from far and wide to be healed by this lovely young girl with the distinctive cornflower blue eyes and fiery red hair. When someone sat down in front of her, impressions and visions washed over Annabel Rose as she started to receive messages. Speaking in a voice twice her size, she would channel advice for their lives, as well as cures for ailments. In an instant, she could help a barren woman fall pregnant, break the fever of a loved one or help heal a farmer's sick horse.

As the news of Annabel Rose's success grew, her father's angry temper started to subside. People were congratulating him on raising such a wonderful daughter. Annabel Rose knew that it had more to do with the money she was bringing in than his admiration for her healing abilities. But there was another wonderful result that happened because of her father's changed behavior. He stopped beating his wife. Margret Mary's tired, battered body started to mend and she was able to slowly regain her strength and health.

With increasing age, Annabel Rose's beauty blossomed and she became quite desirable to many who would have wanted her hand in wedlock. Yet, she would not hear of anything to do with marriage. All her life she had watched her violent father beat her obedient, loving mother mercilessly. The scars from those beatings were not only visible on Margret Mary's body; they had been indelibly stamped on Annabel Rose's soul. She had vowed that she would never marry. Her work as a healer had been quite lucrative all these years and she swore that she would never become beholden to any man.

Annabel Rose not only helped individuals, but it became quite apparent that her healing abilities had a far wider reach, as the health and wellbeing of the whole village started to improve. It was as if a dark cloud had been swept away from the lives of the villagers. As a result of their improved heath and circumstances, they were happier and more productive. With the increase in the amount of their goods, this meant that there was ample money to pay their taxes and keep their larders full for their families. This newfound empowerment led them to take more responsibility and control of their lives.

The recent prosperity of the village had not gone unnoticed by the Baron. Even though he believed that 'a woman should be shown her place in life,' he was more than happy to reap the extra benefits of this renowned healing woman's powers. The village's increased productivity only added to the Baron's wealth, as the villagers were now able to pay their taxes. There was no way that he was going to slaughter this fatted cow.

Yet there was another who did not share the enthusiasm of the Baron.

Annabel Rose's affect on the village did not go unnoticed by the Priest. He no longer had villagers come to him and cry, plead and beg for God's mercy. Their extra offerings that they used to be so quick to give, in order to assure their forgiveness and salvation, had all but dried up. He saw that the people had gained a sense of empowerment and hope, and were no longer in fear of the Church. Scratching his bald head, the Priest thought a Church without fear and control is a very empty Church indeed.

It didn't take the Priest long to find accomplices for his evil plan. Any number of eager, willing thieves could be easily bought for the right price. The Priest told the thieves to watch Annabel Rose carefully and find out the names of those who visited her for healings.

Every week, the Priest had one person murdered. He made sure that herbs and crystals were tossed over the bodies. And on each body, he had his henchmen carve a five pointed star into their chests. There were many who believed that this sign was associated with witches and the occult. And although Annabel Rose never associated her healings with the occult, it is amazing what a hysterical, fearful mob will believe when their lives are in danger. It was after the discovery of the fourth body that an alarm was raised and the frightened villagers met in the town square.

Standing in the middle of the villagers, the Priest calmed the crowd and spoke in a measured, authoritative tone. "Good town's folk, we must try to find out who is the perpetrator of these evil crimes." Looking around the crowd, the Priest then said, "Who knew the victims?"

Slowly a brother, a wife, a mother and a friend stepped forward. When questioned where the murdered victims had been, and whom they had been associating with, it didn't take long for Annabel Rose's name to be attached to each one of the victims.

Feeding the fear of the crowd, the Priest yelled, "This is the work of the Devil and all of the murders lead back to Annabel Rose MacDonald."

The villagers looked around, but Annabel Rose was nowhere in sight. "We must protect ourselves. Go out, one and all, and bring her here for justice to prevail." Grabbing pitchforks, scythes and sticks, the angry mob ran to Annabel Rose's hut.

Sitting quietly beside her favorite stream and looking over the beauty of the lush, verdant fields, Annabel Rose knew that this was her last communion with nature. Closing her eyes, she let the song of the birds rest gently on her heart and she breathed in the deep connection with the energies of the trees. She had foretold this day coming for quite some time, but there was very little that she could have done to stop it. Knowing all this, if she had decided to run, she would not have gotten far. She was guilty of no more than compassionately caring for others. By running, she would have shown the villagers that she was guilty.

As she made her way back to her hut, she said her silent goodbyes to the woods, the animals and the stream that had been her sanctuary for many years. Waiting silently, she breathed deeply and began to pray—not for a different outcome—but for God to give her strength.

Bursting through her door, the enraged villagers bound her hands. Dragging and pushing her outside, they set fire to her hut and yelped in fits of delight. The mob then followed behind, calling for revenge. "Burn the witch! Burn the witch! Get rid of the devil woman!"

Margret Mary watched helplessly as the angry mob dragged Annabel Rose along the dusty dirt road to the village square. Struggling to get to her feet, Annabel Rose stood before the Priest.

"Annabel Rose MacDonald, you stand accused of murder. Did you have these four people come to see you?"

Stoically eyeing the Priest, she replied, "Aye, each came to me for healing and went away improved and healthy. I am only guilty of caring for others and letting God work through me."

"And does God's work include murder?" shouted the Priest.

The villagers cried out, "Murderer! Murderer!"

Quieting the crowd, the Priest then continued, "As I am a holy man of God, I will not cast the first stone. But I will leave it up to the good people of the village who have had their family members murdered to decide your fate."

The silence of the crowd was broken with a sudden uproar and chants of, "Burn the witch! Burn the witch!" The noise from the angry mob drowned out the anguished pleas of Margret Mary to save her daughter. And although Annabel Rose felt a need to defend herself, she knew in her heart that her own pleas would fall on deaf ears. She felt the salty taste of blood as she bit hard into her lip, silencing her words. Running to the forests and chopping down branches, the furious crowd started to pile the wood around a stake in the ground. Tying a rope tightly around Annabel Rose's ankles, they then wrapped the rope around her body several times, binding her to the stake. The ropes bound her feet so tightly that they started to turn blue.

As the branches and dry kindling crackled, the wood fueled the first flames around Annabel Rose's feet. Looking over at her mother, she said "I love you dearly mother. Thank you and may God bless you." As the flames grew stronger, Annabel Rose started to smell her burning flesh and …

5

Heaven—Spirit Hospital

... Suddenly the smell and the pain were completely gone. Looking down at the fireball of human flesh below her, Annabel Rose heard a comforting Scottish voice.

"Me name is Iona; I've come to help you. Come away with me, child. I will take you o're the stream, way down deep in the forest glen where ye can rest and get yer strength back." Anticipating Annabel Rose's question, her guide said, "Don't worry, sweet child. You will be so safe and hidden deep in the thicket of the heather that nobody will ever find you there."

Still emotionally blank from the horrendous ordeal of being burnt alive, Annabel Rose allowed the guide to hold her hand and take her into the tunnel. Upon entering, there was a huge whooshing sound as she was carried along to a bright, white light.

When Iona tenderly looked over to measure Annabel Rose's reactions, all she saw was a blank, frozen expression. Knowing that after her horrific experience she would need intensive care, Iona guided her in a very different direction. Coming to the light at the end of the tunnel, many of the souls began to recognize familiar faces of family and friends who were waiting to be reunited. But Annabel Rose's guide directed her to another area that was specifically designed for those who have experienced deep trauma in their incarnation. Caring angels took Annabel Rose and led her to Spirit Hospital. It was here that they put her in a sleep induced state in an enclosed chamber to help nurture her soul back to health.

For those souls like Annabel Rose, who have endured physical, mental, emotional and/or spiritual torture, this area provides them with the much-needed healing energy that is so important for their recovery. Souls in Spirit Hospital are tenderly comforted, cocooned and looked after in the most loving way. The angels continuously sing healing songs in the angelic language to help lift their damaged energies and fill their souls with much needed light. This process is carried out with a great deal of compassion and everyone is treated with dignity, acceptance, respect and love.

Unlike the Earth plane, no one in Heaven is neglected, shamed or left behind. Having awakened to the realization that we are all One, enlightened beings understand that whatever we do to others, we do to ourselves.

Over time, these souls eventually awaken and are strong enough to go through the transition process. They will be able to be reunited with their family and friends, have homecoming parties, see their pets and go through the orientation process of Heaven. Just like the other souls, they will go to the Hall of Justice and be able to review their incarnation with their newly-healed mind and soul. Afterwards, they will visit the Hall of Akashic Records and review the contract they created in their Book of Life with the Etheric Council.

With great care and loving attention from the angels, Annabel Rose slowly started to heal, and over time, the light within her grew brighter. Her well-being improved so much that her angel guide Iona knew that it was time for Annabel Rose to leave Spirit Hospital and go through the orientation process. Bidding goodbye to the caring angels at Spirit Hospital, Iona and Annabel Rose stepped into a flower-filled garden, rich with radiant colors that burst all around them. The vibrant shades of the flowers spoke directly to Annabel Rose's soul as she reconnected with the energies of nature.

Leaning over to smell one of the enormous blossoms, she came face to face with hundreds of freckles, a tiny nose and the pointiest ears she had ever seen. An extremely tall girl uncurled herself from her crouched position in the flowers and towered over her.

Flicking her long, light brown hair off her face, the girl introduced herself. "Hello there, Annabel Rose. My name is Meaghan. I was your spirit guide when you were on the Earth plane. How are you feeling?"

"I thought Iona was my angel guide," Annabel Rose said.

Meaghan scrunched up her face and said, "She was and so am I. You see, everyone has many angels that help and guide them, but most of the time humans get one special spirit guide assigned to them for life."

Annabel Rose gazed off in the distance. "I used to have a sister named Meaghan, but she was married off when she was very young, and I never met her. But thank you for asking; I am feeling so much better."

"And I am so glad of it!" Iona smiled. "I will be leaving you now but I know that you will be well taken care of by Meaghan." And with those words, she slowly faded from view.

Meaghan picked one of the flowers and put it in her hair. "Aye, it be such a lovely day. Come, let's walk through the forest a wee bit." She seemed to float across the ground as her long green skirt danced on the breeze. She so reminded Annabel Rose of a faerie. Trying not to draw attention, she glanced at Meaghan's pointy ears and tried to look for her wings. Meaghan stopped and laughed, "Ye be right. They are there! But they beat so quick that they can't be seen."

"Why did I choose a faerie to be my spirit guide?" Annabel Rose asked quizzically.

Quickly darting in, out and around the flowers, Meaghan then came to an abrupt stop in mid-air. "Your love of Mother Nature drew us together. I am from the group called the Elementals. The faerie kingdom, along with gnomes, elves, unicorns, devas and many others, look after plants of every description, as well as crystals, rocks and minerals. In essence, Elementals look after anything of the Earth."

"But isn't that the job of the angels?"

Heaving a rather irritated sigh, Meaghan huffed, "Ha! The angels are so busy with their lofty jobs and their heads in the clouds that they do not touch the ground and soil their wings." Scooping up a handful of soil, Meaghan breathed in the earthy aroma, wiped her hands together, and said, "So it is up to us faeries to get down and dirty." Glancing around to make sure no one was listening, she winked at Annabel Rose. "Anyway, faeries get to have so much more fun than angels." As if to prove her point, she darted high into the air and performed a somersault. "And you know Annabel Rose, with your great love for Mother Nature, who better to be your spirit guide than someone who shares your same passion. In that way, you and I are very much alike, as our hearts speak the same language."

Annabel Rose did feel an overwhelming connectivity to this pixie-like girl.

Coming to the edge of the forest, Annabel Rose looked up at the beautiful pink marble building in front of her. Meaghan took her hand and squeezed it tightly. "Here we be at the Hall of Justice, just in time for your screening. When you're finished I will be waiting for you...."

"Amongst the flowers, correct?" said Annabel Rose, quickly finishing her sentence.

"Aye, that's right!" Meaghan smiled and darted away.

Walking in through the stately columned building, Annabel Rose felt a sense of familiarity. As she sat down, a huge holograph appeared and her life review began.

She loved seeing herself playing and snuggling to sleep with her sisters Bonnie, Fiona and Jean. Watching herself spending countless hours in the wooded glen by her house gave her such a warm, secure feeling. She recognized the many villagers who came to her for healings. As the images revealed her life as a healer, she felt honored to be of service doing God's work.

As well as reviewing the pleasant things of her life, she also had to review her challenges and struggles. She winced and recoiled as she watched her father beating her poor mother. She also listened to the Priest's damning and destructive lies against her as his words cut deep into her soul. She watched the final frame of herself tied to a stake surrounded by flames.

As the review of her life ended, Annabel Rose walked out of the Hall and down the marble steps into the courtyard. As promised, Meaghan darted quickly over to her.

"Are you all right, Annabel Rose?"

"Yes, I'm fine."

"Do you need some time before going to the Hall of Akashic Records?"

Annabel Rose thought for a moment and said, "Surprisingly no. I am ready to see the Etheric Council right now."

With the utterance of those words, the Hall began to appear before her. Climbing the steps of the pink marbled building, Annabel Rose walked up the rose steps and into the great Hall where the semicircle of Elders was seated and waiting for her. The Council looked up.

"Hello, Ariel. Welcome back Home. It is wonderful to see you again."

Upon hearing her real name, she replied, "Thank you, dear Council. It is wonderful to be back again."

Opening up her Book of Life, the Elders silently reviewed her contract before speaking in unison.

"That was quite a different life you chose from the previous one. Tell us, Ariel, what you learned."

Ariel took a deep breath. "I wanted to challenge myself to see if I could remember what is important in one's life; especially when one's circumstances are quite harsh."

"Please give us an example."

Pausing for a few moments, Ariel then spoke deliberately. "Unlike my wealthy, privileged life as a Princess in Egypt, this time I chose a life of abject poverty. Having been born into serfdom as a woman in the 1300s gave me no rights and freedoms at all. Yet, within this life, I was more than able to enjoy the love of my mother and siblings. My constant connection with nature gave me a greater feeling of fulfillment and abundance than any of the gold, silver and jewels which were readily mine as Egyptian royalty. Even in my squalid existence, I was able to help others to heal and be of service to God. Drawing the wrath and fury of the Priest and the villagers gave me an opportunity to show conviction and courage to stand up for what I believed in. For this and so much more, I am very proud of my choices."

While she was speaking, a golden glow seemed to encase Ariel and turn to a brilliant white. After a long silence, the Elders spoke. "We can give you no higher accolades than those that you have just given to yourself, Ariel. The compassionate, empowered, loving life of service that you just completed was a reflection in every way of God's Divine word in action." The Elders stood and bowed. "We salute you for your strength and your connection to be of service to God." Presenting a page for her to sign, the Council witnessed her contract with their signatures and closed her Book of Life. "Go and be well Ariel. We know of someone small and furry who can't wait to see you."

Walking out into the garden, Meaghan embraced Ariel. "I hear that you make a great pasta sauce."

Laughing, Ariel said, "Nothing is hidden in Heaven. If you would like, I'll invite you over soon for a taste."

Merely thinking about her villa suddenly made it appear in front of her eyes. The pergola was overflowing with gardenia and jasmine flowers once more. Along the edge of the balcony sprang up the lilac trees and wisteria. The grape arbor lay heavy and her garden groaned under the weight of ripe vegetables waiting to be picked. As the patio's hand painted tiles appeared, the fields of sunflowers quickly painted themselves into the picture as they waved their heads to welcome her back.

Ariel glanced around the patio and said, "Okay, little one, where are you?" She sensed Cleo was hiding and just waiting to surprise her. Entering the kitchen, Ariel thought that some beautiful almond biscotti would taste very nice with a cup of tea. And although she could have instantly manifested the traditional Italian biscuits, she chose to indulge her love of baking instead.

Looking in her pantry, she said aloud, "OK, I'll need some sugar, some yeast, a pinch of salt and some almonds." She laughed and said, "Oh, and of course some flour." Taking off the lid from a large barrel beneath the counter, Cleo jumped out of the barrel and into her arms. Flour went everywhere, but neither of them cared as Ariel was overjoyed to be reunited with her little friend again.

Ariel immersed herself back into her Italian life. It was such a joy to reconnect with the locals and ride her bike through the beautiful, undulating countryside once again. Sitting under the umbrella on her lovely patio, Ariel had a stack of books next to her. Although she always had a love of reading, this time on her return, she felt as if she had been starved of knowledge and it seemed that reading was the only way to quench her hunger. Looking through the titles of her many books, she reminisced about her life as Annabel Rose. It felt horrible to think that most of the population did not know how to read or write. Yet, women especially were denied the right to any education and could only look forward to a life of childbearing and hard labor. With the life expectancy of a woman averaging in the late twenties, if the constant childbearing didn't shorten her life, then the backbreaking hard labor certainly would.

On her return to Home, Ariel instantly knew on which level she wanted to work and she teleported herself to the third level of Heaven. This was the level of animals and plants. With her love of Mother Nature, she wanted to research new medicinal uses for herbs and plants, and the healing energies of minerals and crystals.

Arriving at this level, she heard a familiar Scottish accent.

"I had a feeling you would end up here. I may be a wee bit biased, but this is the best level of all." Darting out from behind a bush, Meaghan flew in a circle and came down next to Ariel. "Come, I've been raving to my friends about the incredibly brave life you just lived and there are some cute leprechauns and elves who are just dying to meet you."

Ariel giggled at her guide's choice of words and matchmaking notions, as Meaghan grabbed Ariel's hand and pulled her into the forest.

After a day spent researching the rainforests and finding out information for alternative and natural forms of medicines, a happy and energized Ariel returned to her villa. Reflecting on her wonderful day, she thought that when people love what they are doing, they never feel burdened by it.

Walking out onto her balcony, Ariel watched the full moon rise over the cypress trees. She reflected on her life back in Heaven. She loved her villa, her friends and working with the plants. Everything was absolutely 'heavenly.' Remembering Meaghan's use of the words 'dying to meet you,' Ariel thought that she must remember to tell Meaghan about her use of the word 'heavenly.' Thinking back to her session with the Etheric Council, Ariel recalled how much the Elders praised her for the life she had just lived.

So why was she so pensive?

"Yoo-hoo, can I come in?" Even before Ariel could think yes, Meaghan flew in through the window and landed on a shelf. "So, you're thinking about returning to Earth already. I say, my girl, you sure are keen and don't waste much time between lives, do you?"

"Well, it's not that," Ariel quickly replied. "I just feel as if I have unfinished business, in some way."

Meaghan gave her a sassy sideward glance. "Be careful what you wish for, girl, because you WILL get it in Heaven." In an instant, both of them were standing in front of the Hall of Akashic Records. Meaghan was wide-eyed and shook a finger at Ariel. "See, I told you so. Now you've gone and done it." Waving goodbye to Meaghan, Ariel advanced up the rose steps and found herself once again in the great Hall.

Glancing over their thick glasses, the Etheric Council had a look of surprise.

"Back so soon? Weren't you just here? What is this all about?"

Ariel spoke with a great deal of conviction. "Perhaps it's because I became empowered in my last life in spite of my harsh conditions, but I felt the great injustice of how women were treated and I would like to go back and live a life of independence, literacy and high education."

Before she knew it, Ariel had verbally painted the portrait of what she wanted to create in her next incarnation. She picked out the era, the continent, her circumstances, her gender, her race, her religion, and the people, family and friends who would help her to learn her lessons on her next chosen human life.

As soon as her signature had been completed on her contract, the Elders closed her Book of Life and said, "I don't think we have ever had anyone who was more enthusiastic about returning to the Earth plane as you, Ariel. Go with the grace of God."

Ariel found herself once again standing on the outgoing platform of the transition level. Looking at all the others who were waiting to descend to Earth, she thought, "I finally know how to pack light." Hearing her thoughts, the others around her smiled.

Within seconds, she was sucked into the tunnel and traveling back to her next Earth incarnation.

6

Venice, Italy, 1531

The gentle lapping of the waves against the side of the gondola made her feel like a baby being rocked in its cradle. Soft velvet seats cushioned Angelica's pampered body. As her gondola glided along the canals of Venice, her outing mixed business with pleasure. Opting for an open gondola, her beauty was freely on exhibit for all to view. Provocatively dressed in an off-the-shoulder, low cut gown, her intentions and her morals left very little to the imagination.

As the gondola slipped under a bridge, she gazed upwards and scanned the people who clung to the sides of the overpass. And while not everyone approved of Courtesans, she was applauded more times than she was jeered. Gentlemen from far and wide had heard about the famous Courtesans of Venice, and they dreamt about catching the eye of one of these renowned, opulent beauties. More esteemed than mistresses, these exquisite, highly paid women were so much more than prostitutes. And rather than being cursed and publically shamed, the majority of men championed their tempting ways and repaid them with extraordinary riches.

Waving to her eager admirers, Angelica mused that she was just as important to the financial welfare of the city as its bustling waterways. It was common knowledge that the ruling elite of Venice would stay intact only if each generation of aristocracy denied marriage to some of their sons. In this way, their family's wealth would not be divided through marriage vows. With eternal bachelorhood thrust upon these privileged men, the Courtesans satisfied their desires without dividing the family's wealth.

The voice of one of her many admirers rose above the crowd. "Angelica, *sei il mio angelo?*"

Hearing her name, the dark-eyed, raven-haired beauty tilted her head up toward the overpass. A single rose had been tossed off the bridge, and it drifted silently into her gondola. Picking up the rose, she shook her long black mane around her shoulders and laughed.

"*Hai bisogno piu d'un grand jardino pieno dei fiori di incontrami. Gratzie, lo stesso.*" Upon hearing that he would need more than a whole garden full of flowers just to meet her, the despondent fellow was mocked and jostled by the crowd.

Smirking to herself, Angelica felt a little sorry for the young man. Maybe in the very early days of her training, she might have given him the time of day; but certainly not now. Her life was filled with rich merchants, bankers, diplomats, and even churchmen. Influential, rich and powerful men all sat at her table, drank in her wit and lay their riches down to bed her.

Closing her eyes, those early days of training flooded over her.

Angelica grew up knowing full well that her mother, Caterina, was a Courtesan. Her mother's life was never hidden in shame, but rather she was renowned for her knowledge and abilities in the ways of pleasuring men. In fact, as little girls, Angelica and her sister Gabriella sat on the steps of their home and watched the passing parade of men in and out of their palazzo. The sisters looked forward to the visits from their mother's suitors, as they would often be spoiled with little gifts and treats.

With the passing years as her mother had gotten older, the number of suitors had started to diminish. Caterina knew how much money that she still had left for her family's survival and, unless she took action, there would only be enough to see them through for a few more years.

Giggling coming from outside suddenly interrupted Caterina's thoughts. Walking out to the balcony, she watched her daughters at play in the courtyard below. She had spent the better part of the last sixteen years preparing them in the ways to attract a rich husband. They were taught social graces and how to dress, dance, play the piano, sing and embroider. Caterina knew that a girl's efforts to catch a husband were supposed to be subtle and understated. In fact, by a girl appearing more naïve in the ways of the world, she somehow seemed more needy and, therefore, seen as less of a threat.

In this strange way, a girl's dependency became her best asset to obtain a husband. For it was a girl's innocence and her limited knowledge of politics and finances that made her vulnerable and in need of a man to look after her. An obedient girl would be passed from her controlling father to her controlling new husband and she would submit willingly. She would never question his superiority and would be subservient in fulfilling all his desires.

Like her own family, Caterina was neither wealthy enough to keep her daughters at home forever, nor did she have the money for a large dowry to entice prospective suitors into marrying them. Shivering at the thought of her daughters working as char women and getting old before their time, Caterina knew there were only two other avenues open to sixteen-year-old Gabriella and fifteen-year-old Angelica.

First, if she were lucky enough to use her connections as a Courtesan, Caterina might be able to get them jobs as governesses. Gabriella certainly showed a great deal of patience and loved playing with children. But Caterina knew that securing a job as a governess had very little to do with a girl's ability to look after children and more to do with who one knew.

The second option was for the girls to be sent off to a convent to live out their lives as nuns. Hardly the life she would have envisaged for any daughter of hers.

Breathing a huge sigh, Caterina would have loved for her girls to experience true, romantic love. Yet when all was said and done, a girl's feelings and her preferences in the matter of love were irrelevant. Caterina knew that marriage was no more than a contract and not based on romantic feelings. Weddings were but a thinly veiled financial agreement arranged to benefit a young woman's family while conferring prestige on the other party. No more, no less.

Having come to a decision, Caterina leaned over the balcony and called down to the courtyard for her daughters to come into the house. Bursting through the doorway, the girls raced in and fell onto the sofa. Fidgeting and giggling, they were flushed from their wild play and the redness in their cheeks made them appear like dolls.

Gabriella was as fair as Angelica was dark. Her long, golden blonde hair and fair skin, thanks to her mother's blonde, blue-eyed suitor, was such a contrast to her sister's olive complexion. It was quite common for Courtesans to have children and, many times, different lovers fathered them.

In addressing the girls, Caterina spoke openly about the family's financial position. She went on to explain that through the kind favor of the Emperor—who had known her charms repeatedly over many years—she was almost certain that she could entice him to take one of the girls on as a governess.

Gazing lovingly at both of her daughters, Caterina spoke. "The choice that I have made is not an easy one, but it is the only one that will save the family from penury." Walking around the table and taking Gabriella's hands, she said, "You have always been such a bright, willing child; always happy to please others. Your contented disposition will do you very well when looking after children."

Gabriella started to cry, for she knew that she would be sent far away and might never see her mother or her sister again.

Turning to Angelica, Caterina carefully chose her words.

"Angelica, you would have done well to have had a father to teach you some discipline. Unlike Gabriella's quiet countenance, you have always been rebellious, setting out to prove yourself to others in a high, arrogant manner. Well, my dear, we will take that lofty opinion that you hold for yourself and put it to good use for our family's benefit. I have decided that you will carry on the grand tradition of being a Courtesan."

Angelica's dark eyes glared defiantly at her mother.

Grabbing her daughter's chin, Caterina sternly said, "Yes, those high cheek bones and grand nature of yours will be much sought after in the years to come."

Putting all her efforts into her younger daughter, Caterina educated Angelica in the art of the Courtesan. Every aspect of her waking moments was carefully scrutinized. She was taught to speak with an upper class accent, schooled in the art of lavish dressing, and shown how to fashionably arrange her hair. Her knowledge of jewels and precious gems was broadened and she was soon able to distinguish ordinary gemstones from priceless ones.

All areas of poise, manners and protocols on how to act were carefully practiced. In addition to being taught social manners and many forms of dance, Angelica perfected her ability to play the piano and to sing.

One of her greatest challenges was to walk on the elevated shoes called *chopines*. These shoes were not only created to keep the long dresses of the Venetian women out of the mud, but they also gave the Courtesans an air of heightened superiority as their heads teetered above the crowds.

Over the next several years, Angelica matured into a breathtaking woman. And while she tolerated all of the concentration on her outward appearance, there was only one aspect of her transformation that she was absolutely passionate about. As Courtesan, she was allowed access to the libraries of Venice.

She loved that she was allowed to read, acquire knowledge and expand her education. As a companion to noblemen, dukes and princes, she had to be well versed in the plots of operas, recognize literary references and be familiar with history and politics. As her clientele would often be multi-lingual, she became adept at learning many languages and the nuances of different cultures. Once her skills were honed to perfection, her mother thought to arouse some interest in her and took Angelica out on her sixteenth birthday.

It took the better part of the whole day to bathe, make-up and coif an elaborate hairstyle for Angelica's first outing in almost a year. Standing in front of a mirror, Caterina arranged her daughter's frilly linen undergarments. Angelica's low cut silk bodice was so tight, the crisscrossing of the ribbons in the front of the gown only allowed her to take shallow breaths. Running her fingers over the material of the bodice, Angelica smiled as she felt the fine embroidery of the silver threads and tiny pearl beads. Edging the top of her bodice, like a beautiful frame, was the most exquisite lace from Burano. Caterina had made a trip to the tiny island to have the beautiful lace specially made for her daughter's dress.

Next, the delicately embroidered puffed sleeves were tied on with ribbons. This invention of detachable sleeves provided women with a wider range of wardrobe choices.

Caterina then grabbed the skirt and put it over Angelica's head. The beautiful blue waves of color unfolded as it drifted full length to the floor. Cinching the skirt around her waist, Angelica was forced to breathe in even more, which made her turn almost the same shade of blue as the material on the skirt, She realized why Courtesans had to always be accompanied by escorts; as they were in constant danger of collapsing from the lack of oxygen.

Taking a silver jewelry box down off a shelf, Caterina looked through her collection of exquisite gems for just the right color. As her fingers lightly touched the sparkling jewels, they rekindled wonderful memories of the admiration of many suitors. Finally settling on a diamond and sapphire set that had been given to her by the Emperor himself, Caterina put the finishing touches on her daughter's outfit.

Angelica then slipped her rose-colored stocking feet into a pair of beautiful shoes that her mother placed in front of her. Their tops were embroidered in the same blue as the skirt and their heels were ten inches high. Angelica stared at herself in the mirror.

Caterina then handed her daughter a gold-trimmed, tasseled fan. Upon opening the fan, Angelica grinned as it revealed risqué images of a naked man and woman entwined.

As she draped a dark blue silk scarf precariously over Angelica's soft, bare shoulders, Caterina stepped back and took a long, careful look at her creation.

She was very pleased as she smiled to herself. She knew that to succeed as a Courtesan meant that a woman not only had to be beautiful, sophisticated and elegant in dress and manner, but more importantly, she had to be an eloquent and cultivated conversationalist. She felt that Angelica was more than ready in all areas.

Having overseen her daughter's every lesson, Caterina knew that she was well taught. Yet, she also knew that education alone does not make an interesting bed partner and that there was nothing that could teach one better than practical experience.

Hiding her smile from Angelica, Caterina thought that her daughter's independent streak and unbridled spirit would finally be a blessing for her. She knew that the best Courtesans must have an elusive air that made them seem like rare, exotic birds to men. And while there were many who would love to gaze at and capture these exquisite creatures, they need to be wild and free or, once captured, they would quickly die in captivity.

Taking her daughter's soft, delicate hand, Caterina lead Angelica into the waiting gondola to take them to St. Mark's Square. When Angelica's beautifully embroidered slipper stepped onto the dock, little did Caterina realize how renowned her daughter would become as one of Venice's most famous and prized Courtesans. Over the next ten years, it was not only her beauty that was courted and bedded by many influential men of power and wealth; she was also prized for her intellect. With her vast knowledge of history, politics and foreign affairs, she was often the only woman asked to advise and sit counsel among heads of state.

In this way, along with great wealth, Angelica had gone on to amass notoriety as she had become one of the most highly educated women in all of Europe.

The sounds of children's laughter along the canal brought

Angelica back to the present moment and her gondola ride. Watching the children at play made her think about her own childhood as she fondly remembered the carefree, innocent days with her sister Gabriella. She imagined what her life might have been like had she been chosen as a governess instead of her sister.

With the sudden bump of the gondola against the dock of her beautiful palazzo, her thoughts turned to her evening plans. Grabbing the hand of a waiting servant, she teetered into her magnificent receiving room. Walking past the richly-decorated frescoed and *trompe l'oeil* walls, she stepped into her salon and eased herself into a plush sofa. The room was appointed with the finest of antiques, and priceless tapestries draped the walls. Reaching for a tiny porcelain bell on the inlaid mother-of-pearl table, Angelica rang for her maid.

A heavyset gray-haired woman came in with a silver tray holding a delicate hand-painted china tea service. The intoxicating smell of espresso accompanied some beautifully decorated pastries. Gently placing the tray beside her, the maid servant handed her an envelope and a beautiful bouquet of flowers.

"Bounasera, Signorina Angelica. Che un signor, davanti. Lui volgia parlare con te."

Untying the pink ribbon around the envelope, Angelica read the enclosed note and smiled to herself. Lifting up a pink meringue and putting it delicately to her lips, Angelica decided to ignore the fact that she had just been told that a gentleman was wishing to see her, for this was nothing new. Her schedule was already quite full and she had stopped seeing casual callers, along with taking one-night stands, a very long time ago.

Looking into the gilded mirror on the wall, she admired her reflection. She was glad that she had not succumbed to dying her dark hair blonde as many Courtesans did. It gave her originality and made her stand out from the others.

Seeing the long shadows on the richly-appointed hand woven rugs told Angelica that dusk was drawing near. Remembering the day of the week, Angelica knew that Friday meant she would be seeing

Franco tonight. Being a wealthy merchant, he was always surprising her with gifts and trinkets from foreign lands.

Popping another meringue into her mouth, Angelica was greatly appreciative to all her patrons. Her seven wealthy lovers filled the days of the week and they all paid her a handsome monthly salary for the right to exclusivity. And for their money they expected much more than just sex. She basically replaced their wives, since proper married women were sequestered from the sins of the world and often kept prisoners in their own homes. Yet, unlike a secret liaison with a mistress, Courtesans were proudly displayed and expected to accompany their different lovers to events, parties and balls.

Angelica even hosted gatherings of her lovers' friends at her own home. She was very proud of her accomplishments and numbered kings, regents and painters as her friends. Gazing up at the wall, she saw the magnificent portrait that Tintoretto had painted of her.

Climbing the steps to her second floor, Angelica undressed and stepped carefully into an already-prepared perfumed bath. Lying back in the rose-petal waters, she eased herself into the warmth as thoughts of her mother washed over her.

Auctioning off her sixteen-year-old daughter's virginity to the highest bidder was a wonderful idea of Caterina's. It heightened the men's arousal as the competition for the eventual winner drove the price higher. Being paraded and admired by so many prospective suitors was at first flattering to Angelica. Yet, when the fateful day arrived, with the highest bidder handing over a great roll of money and gold coins into her mother's hand, Angelica suddenly had a change of heart.

When the scheduled night of the exchange of goods and services finally arrived, Angelica tried to fight off her suitor's advances with all her might and she scratched his face. As little beads of blood started forming streaks across his cheek, he chuckled and was spurred on by the challenge of a fight. In the end, her delicate frame was no match for the strength of the wealthy banker. Being a member of one of the most powerful banking families in Italy, he always got whatever he wanted. Picking her up and violently hurling Angelica onto the bed, he held her down with one massive hand and thrust himself into her.

Biting down hard on her lip, so hard that she could taste blood, she held back the tears. It was then that she vowed, from that day forward, she would become the most renowned Courtesan in order to control men and command their respect.

Shaking her head to clear the painful memory away, she returned her thoughts to her perfumed bath. Picking up the soft washcloth, she tried to wash away this painful memory by caressing her limbs. Suddenly a vision of Stefano entered her mind. It had been years since she had allowed herself to remember this beautiful young man. His deep brown eyes and curly head of hair was as clear an image as it had been that night when she first saw him.

The year before Caterina had told Angelica that she would be trained to become a Courtesan, she and her two daughters excitedly attended the Venetian festival of Carnivale. As they made their way through the crowded streets, Angelica took off her mask and immediately locked eyes with a dark-eyed, handsome young man. Time stood still for both of them as an unseen energy instantly drew them to one another. At the shared age of fourteen their love was pure, affectionate and innocent. With their hearts bursting with joy, they cared not about finances, alliances and social standing. All they cared about was being together.

Having made up her mind about her daughter's future life as Courtesan, Caterina forbade Angelica to see him. As their love was so strong, Angelica and Stefano continued to see one another in secret; while hiding their meetings from Caterina.

Hearing her daughter sneaking in late one night, Caterina knew that she had no other choice. A boyfriend was not to be tolerated and would greatly hamper the allure of a Courtesan. Using her influential connections, Caterina had Stefano conscripted into the army and transported far away from Venice; and far away from Angelica.

Roughly pushing away the rose petals as she pushed away the memory of her beloved Stefano, she stepped from her bath. She dried herself, put on a robe of the finest silk and sat at her dressing table.

While applying her make-up, she had a vivid memory of both herself and Gabriella watching her mother prepare herself for the arrival of one of her mother's many suitors. She smiled as she remembered pleading with her mother to allow them to put on some make-up and try on her clothes. Despite both sisters' attempts to remain standing as they tried on their mother's high shoes, they laughed uncontrollably as they fell over on top of one another. They would watch their exasperated mother try to keep her composure as she fought back her own laughter.

Feeling the burning tears starting to form, Angelica thought, "My God, how I miss my beloved mother and sister." It had been years since she received the news of Gabriella's death from smallpox. Being a master of controlling her emotions, Angelica took a deep breath, composed herself and forced the tears and memories back into the past.

Opening her robe, Angelica studied the lines of her beautiful body. As her hands touched her stomach, a chill swept over her. Her mother had always been so careful about Angelica taking precautions so that she would not fall pregnant. Closing her robe to banish the chill, she wondered what would have happened if her mother had been alive on that misty, cold morning when she had made her fateful decision.

Angelica recalled that January years ago as she braced herself for the journey along the damp city streets. Tucking an additional blanket around her already well-wrapped bundle, she ventured out into the early morning fog. The icy wind blowing off the canal made her grab the collar of her coat and pull it even tighter around her. The biting cold on that day reminded Angelica of the winter's day two years previously when she had buried her mother.

Making her way down to the sea to St. Marks Street, a shiver ripped through her body. Observing the street numbers as she walked down the winding *calle*, Angelica knew the precise directions that the servant girl had given her, along with the description of the building that she sought.

All of a sudden, she turned a corner and there it was. She had been told that there was no sign, only an iron gate inserted into a hollow piece of the wall. There was just enough room to place an infant child up to the age of about two months. This house for bringing up bastard children was set up specifically to deal with all the unwanted offspring of the Courtesans.

Putting down her basket, Angelica opened up the blanket and peered inside. Not even one week old, her baby daughter looked so much like herself. Steeling herself for what must be done, she rewrapped her daughter in an extra blanket, opened the gate, put the little girl into the vacant space and rang the bell. Quickly running away down the slippery side street, Angelica knew that the nuns on the other side of the wall would take good care of her daughter. And in an instant, she was discharged of all her duties as a mother. She would never have to subject any child of hers to prostitute herself in order to survive.

Glancing at her reflection in her vanity table mirror, she saw the tracks of tears as she remembered her beautiful daughter. And as quickly as the tears came, she regained her tough exterior and wiped her eyes. Grabbing her powder and rouge she said aloud, "I've got more important things to concentrate on now." She reassured herself that her life was full, and there simply was no room for a child. After all, she had her duties to attend to. It was her diligence within her profession that helped her to amass a large fortune. She smiled, knowing that in the years before Caterina died, her mother wanted for nothing.

Sighing deeply, Angelica examined her twenty-six-year-old face and thought that maybe she had another few years still left in her. And although twenty-six was old for a Courtesan, her reputation did precede her. She knew that one's circumstances were not dependent on what you knew, but on who you knew. In any event, her wealth surpassed that of some of her patrons, as she owned a number of townhouses, chateaus and property. Her collection of diamonds and jewels, antiques and other rich furnishings rivaled that of many Venetian noblewomen.

Lying down upon an embroidered gold silk quilt under her white lace canopy, Angelica took a deep breath from her perfumed bed linens and sighed. For all her wealth and the open adoration of men, Angelica had lived a very lonely life. She had never known what it was like to have the deep companionship of other women as friends. Closeness with other Courtesans meant competition for the same patrons. And she couldn't really become friends with noblewomen because she was sleeping with their husbands.

She rang the bell for her maidservant to help her dress for the evening. The gold threads in her gown made her olive skin shimmer. Putting on her waist-length pearls, Angelica heard the servants announce Franco's arrival. Sighing deeply, Angelica thought, "Another ball, another glittering night." Taking one last look in the mirror, she wondered what her life would have been like had she run away with Stefano.

Grabbing her fan, she walked to the balcony. Leaning over, she said, "*Ciao, Franco amore mio. Sono pronta.*" And with that, she glided out of the door of her beautiful palazzo.

Angelica was one of the lucky Courtesans to have lived an opulent, adored life before the wrath of the Inquisition reigned down upon so many in that era. Retiring from her glittering life at the age of thirty, Angelica lived out her days in her magnificent palazzo in the fairytale setting of Venice.

At the age of thirty-five, she contracted an infectious fever that saw her bedridden and depleted of strength. As her servants mopped her perspiring brow, they heard her talking to her mother, Caterina. They attributed it to the delusion of the high fever. But Angelica was in fact conversing with her mother, who was waiting by her bedside. Taking her last breath, Angelica slipped away and found herself in the company of her beloved mother.

"Ciao, mia tesora. Andiamo insieme."

Lovingly embracing her mother, they stepped into the tunnel and made their way once more to the waiting portal of Paradiso.

7

Heaven—Twin Flames

Arriving at the end of the tunnel, the ladies stepped into the white light and onto a pier at St Mark's Square. A nearby group of men bowed as they admired their stunning gowns and finery.

Hidden behind their feathered, bejeweled masks, the two ladies made their way through the crush of people who had gathered to celebrate Carnevale di Venezia. Originally started in 1162 to honor a victory of the Republic of Venice, the festival had not changed very much and it saw people taking to the streets to celebrate in grand jubilation.

The usual darkness of the Piazza San Marco was transformed into light with hundreds of lanterns illuminating the square. Their brightness was increased by the competing fireworks, which were lighting up the sky. As Caterina and Angelica gracefully made their way through the crowd, they saw beloved souls; both family and friends, who had crossed over. The smiles on their faces conveyed the joy in their hearts as they danced to the music and reveled in being reunited once again.

Yet, unbeknownst to them, someone was watching their party from the shadows. Waiting for the music to end, a tall, masked gentleman walked directly over to Caterina, bowed, and asked her permission to dance with Angelica. Sensing only good intentions, Caterina stepped aside and gave the young man permission.

Held in the dancer's embrace, Angelica's body shivered as she felt energy from the gentleman that was both comforting and strangely familiar. As the music ended, he gently lifted Angelica's mask before removing his own. Immediately upon seeing his face, Angelica recognized this handsome gentleman as her beloved Stefano. With tears in their eyes, they fell into each other's arms and deeply embraced. But unlike their teenage tears of forced separation, these tears were full of joy.

Stefano kissed her sweetly on her forehead. *"Com'e stai bella mia?"*

"Tutto posto adesso, amore mio." (Everything's all right now, my love.) With all the men Angelica had been with, the only true feelings of love that she had ever felt were for her beloved Stefano.

"Come, let us walk for a while," said Stefano, taking her hand. "There is so much to say." As they walked away from the square, they meandered down the narrow side streets and stopped on a bridge. Stefano placed a loving hand on Angelica's cheek. "Although we were together only a short while on Earth, I have been watching over you from Heaven." Noticing Angelica's bewildered gaze, he continued, "I have been your spirit guide ever since I was killed in battle."

Shocked, Angelica said, "But I thought that girls would have other girls as spirit guides."

Stefano laughed, "That's not always the case. Just as we choose the country, the race and the culture we want to experience, we can choose our own gender as well as the gender of our Spirit Guides. We need to garner our lessons from as many different perspectives as possible."

As they walked along, the scenery began to change. With every footstep they took, beautiful flowers and plants started to appear. As the winding streets of Venice began to disappear and fragrant hanging gardens formed in front of them, Angelica had an overwhelming sense of familiarity. Suddenly, she froze.

"I know where we are going. I have to go to the Hall of Justice to review my life and then on to meet the Etheric Council in the Hall of Akashic Records."

Stefano smiled. "Your powers of higher perception are coming back quickly."

Hanging her head in embarrassment and shame, Angelica started to weep. "I don't want to review my life. I just want to forget it. I can't possibly share my deep shame with the Etheric Council." Instantly, Angelica heard a familiar voice, which brought tears to her eyes.

"Sisters can do anything just as long as they stick together."

Turning around, Angelica saw the open, loving arms of her sister Gabriella. Hugging her tightly, Gabriella said, "I have been told that they will make an exception and allow me to sit with you during your life's review." Upon uttering those words, they found themselves standing on the familiar pink marbled steps. Steeling herself for her review, Angelica took her sister's hand and started to ascend the steps to the Hall of Justice.

As both girls positioned themselves upon the marble bench in the great Hall, Angelica clung tightly to Gabriella's hand as she watched her life replayed before her eyes. Flinching as she watched countless men share her company and her bed, she felt ashamed and degraded. Watching the way she belittled and mocked others, she felt the hurt caused by her stinging remarks.

At the end of her review, Angelica's heart was heavy with sadness. Exiting the great Hall, the sisters walked into the rose garden. Sensing the deep pain in Angelica's heart, Gabriella touched her on the shoulder.

"My dear one, this is where I will have to leave you, as the Etheric Council has decreed that you must attend to your contract's review solely on your own. Be strong, *corragio.*" Waving farewell to her sister, Gabriella slowly faded from view.

In that instant, Angelica found her feet standing on the marble steps of the Hall of Akashic Records. Breathing out a deep sigh, she slowly began to ascend the wide steps. As she walked through the door, the pounding of her heart seemed to echo through the Hall. With her head down, she hesitantly approached the semi-circle of the Etheric Council. Sensing her deep shame, the Council spoke.

"Hello, dearest Ariel, it is wonderful to see you back with us once more."

Upon hearing her true name, Ariel knew once again who she really was. The Etheric Council opened Ariel's Book of Life and addressed her.

"Tell us, Ariel, about your last human incarnation and experiences on Earth."

Bursting into tears, she began to cry. "Oh beloved Elders, I lived such a terrible life of whoring. I should have run away with Stefano when I had the chance. But with Gabriella gone, there was nobody to look after our mother. I can't understand how I can be forgiven and ever loved again when I prostituted my whole life in such a disgraceful manner." Putting her head in her hands, she wept bitterly.

The Council then spoke to her in a loving, kind manner.

"Dear sweet one, we are not here to judge you, nor condemn you. You say you lived a life of shame. There is no shame in taking care of and providing for a parent. Neither is there any shame in doing whatever you have to do in order to survive. In this way, your life as a Courtesan showed extraordinary strength of character and resilience. In the era in which you chose to live, a woman had little to no rights at all."

Glancing over the contract of her life, the Council continued.

"You wrote in your contract that you wanted to be independent, well-educated and respected. Ariel, if you take a good look at your life, you fully completed that contract."

Allowing these words to settle on Ariel's heart, the Council paused, and then said lovingly, "God does not judge us. Throughout every life, each soul will bring to themselves challenges and experiences to help them grow spiritually. Within all of our challenges, we have free will to make choices in our lives. It is the strength and character that we demonstrate once we have made those choices that matters most in our lives."

With those comforting words of wisdom, the overwhelming weight of sadness started to lift off of her soul. Ariel started to smile as she stood up straight and a heavy burden shifted from her heart.

"Remember, Ariel," the Council reassured her, "God does not condemn anyone no matter what they have done. In fact, there is nothing that anyone can choose to do that will make this Divine, eternal Source stop loving them." Tears welled up in Ariel's eyes.

"Thank you so very much."

"Thank you, Ariel. You did well in completing your contract."

After Ariel and the Etheric Council signed her contract, they closed her Book of Life.

Walking down the steps, Ariel looked around the garden.

"Are you looking for me?"

Ariel turned to see Stefano waiting expectantly for her. Smiling a knowing smile, she said, "Your real name is not Stefano, is it?"

Upon hearing her words, the young man's outer appearance began to change.

"No, Ariel, it's me, Kiel."

On seeing Kiel's smiling face, Ariel beamed as she felt the immense surge of love that bonds Twin Flames. Kiel gently picked up her delicate little hand, put it to his lips, and softly kissed her. His tears of joy reflected the overwhelming feeling of being reunited with his Divine complement.

"Welcome back, my beloved Princess."

The radiance from Kiel's face was a mirror image of the joy emanating from Ariel's heart. Slowly melting into one another, they tenderly enfolded in each other's arms, nestled the sides of their faces together and felt divinely whole once again.

Both Kiel and Ariel knew the extraordinary nature of a Twin Flame relationship, as Twin Flames are more than soul mates. A soul may be reunited with thousands of soul mates in one lifetime to help them along their journey or to clear their karmic debt. Yet a Twin Flame is that singular soul who divinely completes us and there is only one in any space, time and dimension. Kiel knew that Ariel was the female version of him; as Ariel knew that Kiel was the male version of her.

Twin Flames think alike, act alike and finish each other's sentences, and in many instances, they look alike. When Twin Flames finally find each other, many liken the extraordinary experience to returning to a deep peace and joy in their hearts. This blissful connection of being reunited with your Twin Flame has been experienced as coming Home to God.

And while the Twin Flame relationship is romantic in nature, these Twins come together for a higher purpose. Once each of the Twins has become enlightened and self-realized, their energies work like very strong magnets to be drawn together. The fundamental reason for the Twin Flame connection on the Earth plane is to bring forth a mission of God. By marrying the gifts and talents of one Twin with the gifts and talents of the other, these high vibrational, light-filled projects are launched on the Earth plane and help others to be filled with the same love and light in which they were created.

Being reunited with one's Twin Flame when one passes from the physical to the non-physical is not unusual as our vibrations and energies are higher in Heaven, yet this is not the case on Earth. As souls choose to return to Earth to learn their lessons, they have to overcome the many challenges and trials of learning their lessons in the lower dimensional energies of duality. Transcending and enlightening one's vibration is a daily challenge when the majority of the energies around you can be very dense. For Twin Flames to find each other in just such an environment as Earth, they have to be vibrating energetically at the same, extraordinarily high frequency energy waves. This is why it is a rare occurrence for people to find their Twin Flame on the Earth plane.

Feeling the weariness in his beloved's soul, Kiel took Ariel's hands.

"You need to rest, relax and recoup. Where would you like to go?"

Instead of her beautiful Italian villa in the Tuscan hills, Ariel immediately recognized a strong smell of seaweed and heard a familiar crashing of waves along a shoreline.

Nodding his head in agreement, Kiel quickly said, "I didn't want to influence you, but our first house we shared together holds so many dear memories."

Ariel smiled. "I can't think of any place that I would rather be."

And with that thought, the two of them were standing in front of two huge stone pillars that supported shining black iron gates. As they approached, the gates began to swing open. A road painted itself into the picture with a forest of huge maples, elms and oak trees on either side. Squirrels scurried back and forth collecting the bountiful supply of acorns.

Walking down the road, Kiel and Ariel saw a family of deer grazing in the forest. They both laughed, as they knew that the spiritual meaning of the deer is to be gentle with oneself, rest and not push nor hurry life. As they rounded a bend in the road, there in front of them was an enormous four-story Victorian home overlooking the sandy shores of Long Island, New York. These "grand dames," often called Painted Ladies, were named because of their elaborate multi-colored paintwork. With a steady, sweeping glance, Ariel saw the huge expanse of perfectly-manicured, lush green grass spreading far away and nudging the dunes of the beach. Looking to her right, symmetrically trimmed hedges appeared and interconnected to form a maze.

Quickly glancing left, Ariel remembered one of her favorite places to sit and restore her balance and peace. A pink and gray, ornately-carved gazebo covered in lilacs overlooked Long Island Bay. The delicate soft lavender against the pink created a restful combination to while away a lazy afternoon with a book or two; or more.

"Are you ready to go inside?" said Kiel.

"I can't wait," said Ariel.

Their footsteps towards the house prompted stairs to magically appear, beckoning them to climb up to the wide wrap-around porch. Highly glazed white wicker furniture, along with a porch swing, seemed to bid them welcome. The swing was filled with rose chintz pillows and a pink throw blanket, and it moved gently back and forth to entice an eager participant to come and get cozy.

Pushing open the large, carved wooden doors, they both stepped into a grand foyer with fourteen-foot ceilings. The wooden paneling and richly carved banister of the winding staircase gleamed with a highly polished combination of lemon and beeswax. Behind the staircase, rising thirty-feet in the air, were stained-glass windows depicting religious themes. The spectacular beauty of the workmanship was overwhelming.

Stepping right, Ariel entered the grand salon with its elaborate cornice work and floral borders gracing the chair rails. The dark chocolate Chesterfield leather lounge and matching chairs, along with the shiny ebony grand piano, gave the room an air of sophisticated elegance. This room, which featured one of the sunniest spots of the house, had a large bay window. Its brightly colored cushions also seemed to call for someone to come and have some quiet reflection.

Entering the hall, Ariel walked towards the staircase and looked into the grand dining room with its elegant crystal chandelier and mirrored walls. As she quietly went up the stairs, she remembered their treasured sanctuary. Opening the door to the master bedroom, there appeared a white, hand-carved four-poster canopy bed. Each of the four corners of the bed was carved with the delicate features of angels' faces; their flowing, feathery wings wrapping around the posts. Appointed all in white, this heavenly bed looked out over the water. The ceiling was painted in *trompe l'oeil* to depict the clouds in Heaven, while angels and cherubs clung to the walls and sweetly smiled down.

Sensing the weariness of her Earth incarnation melting away, she felt overwhelmed by her many blessings. In that moment, Ariel was distracted by a scratching noise outside in the hall. As she opened the door to investigate the sound, a bundle of fur leapt into her arms.

"My Cleo, oh how I have missed you!" The excited little pooch madly licked Ariel's face. Turning to Kiel, Ariel said, "Let's all go down and watch God's handiwork as the sun sets."

Nestling themselves in the beautiful pink gazebo, the Twins snuggled side by side with Cleo on Ariel's lap. They watched the sky turn fiery red, orange, hazy yellow and then fade to lavenders and dusty pinks. Against this backdrop of heavenly splendor, the Twin Flames melted into each other as their hearts beat rhythmically in time, as one.

These days of being reunited with her beloved Kiel were magical. Every day, they would take a walk with Cleo along the white, powdery sands of their beach and search for treasures from the sea. Their efforts were always rewarded, as Ariel collected brightly colored shells and stones that she incorporated into her artwork.

Her art studio, which used to be a room known as a widow's walk, was a favorite spot. This ocean-facing room had a large expanse of windows, and a large telescope was a constant fixture. Traditionally, the wives and sweethearts of the men who went to sea could look through the telescope and try to catch a precious glimpse of their loved ones returning home. Ariel chose this room as her art studio because she always felt an air of expectancy; as if there was something about to burst forth just beyond the horizon.

Now and again she thought fondly about her Italian villa. But if she had to be truthful, it was here that she felt most complete. This was evidenced by the amount of creativity that spilled forth in her artwork since she had returned Home. Not only was she painting, but she was composing beautiful melodies as well.

Although she was nourished with love, purpose and passion, she sensed that there was some aspect of her growth needed attention. At first it seemed to be a quiet whisper on the breeze, but, after awhile, it became louder with a greater sense of urgency.

It was a hot summer's afternoon as Kiel and Ariel strolled along their familiar beach. They watched as Cleo ran in and out of the waves. Feeling her own waves of emotion building up inside of her, Ariel stopped and turned to Kiel.

"Kiel, I have heard the calling of my soul. I've known in my heart, that there would be a need for greater spiritual growth and awareness. I have been so happy here with you."

Kiel looked lovingly at Ariel. "I am not surprised that you say that, my dear Princess. For it has been some time that I too have had the same yearning for spiritual advancement. I guess we truly are part of the same Divine essence."

Laughing out loud at how similar they were, Kiel said, "I guess I hadn't mentioned anything, because I didn't want to be parted again."

Ariel embraced Kiel and said, "You know we are eternally one and what may seem like a lifetime on Earth, will only be a short amount of time here."

Kiel smiled and nodded his head in agreement.

Breathing a huge sigh Ariel said, "I will leave for the Etheric Council tomorrow."

Saying goodbye to her beautiful seaside home, Ariel stood in the pink gazebo with Kiel and Cleo looking out toward the ocean. "I love you both so dearly. I promise to be back soon." Turning her thoughts to the Hall of Akashic Records, Kiel, Cleo and their beautiful Victorian home slowly started to fade away and the pink marbled steps of the Hall appeared in front of Ariel once more.

As she walked through the doors, she saw the familiar semi-circle of wise faces welcoming her. The Etheric Council said, "Why, hello, Ariel. We have been expecting you for awhile. We know how difficult it is for you to leave your beloved Twin Flame, Kiel. You certainly are dedicated to enlightenment on your path of spiritual growth."

Ariel said, "Something has been weighing on my heart for a while now. My life as Courtesan was one of great wealth and privilege as I had every advantage to a life of freedom with great influence and power.

"What burdens my soul is that, with this great influence and power, I did nothing to help others who were less fortunate than me. I treated my servants with haughty disdain and it never occurred to me to treat them with kindness or even share a small amount of my good fortune with my dedicated, loyal staff. In addition, I looked down upon and ridiculed the submissive, acquiescent wives of the men that I was sleeping with. I never thought of their lack of freedom, as they were betrothed against their wills into marriages not for love; but because of wealthy connections and powerful alliances."

Listening very carefully, the Etheric Council then spoke.

"Ariel, it is never for us to tell you what to do. What action does your soul want to take?"

Ariel spoke with courage. "I want to write in my next contract that I feel what it feels like to be treated with such ill regard and to know what it is to have my freedom taken away."

Hesitantly opening up Ariel's Book of Life, the Etheric Council began to write down every detail that Ariel wanted to include in her contract for her next life.

With great concern, the Council said, "Are you sure that this is the life of your choosing?"

Ariel then spoke with a great deal of conviction. "Yes, I am sure. It is so blatantly clear in Heaven that we are all connected and what one does towards another, one does to oneself. I need to experience what others felt as a result of my lack of compassion and empathy for the people around me."

The Council said, "We are very proud of you and we could not have stated it better ourselves. You are indeed a brave soul to contract such a life." Picking up the long quill pen, they signed her contract, and closed her Book of Life.

As Ariel stood on the platform of the transition level waiting to descend once again to Earth, she closed her eyes and thought of her beloved Kiel. Feeling a soft brush of a kiss against her cheek, she opened her eyes and he appeared before her.

"Going my way?" he said with a cheeky grin.

Bursting out laughing, Ariel replied, "I know that the next incarnations we have chosen are not in the same time period. But I'll catch you later on the flip side." Right before they both stepped into the tunnel, Ariel whispered, "I love you Kiel."

Kiel smiled. "I adore you, my Princess."

With those words settling on her heart, she heard the far off sound of drumming, calling her to experience and learn from another life.

8

Nigeria, Africa/ Virginia, America, 1763

Sitting quietly as her aunt cornrowed her thick, wiry hair, Adetoun felt very special indeed. The crowded hut was overflowing with the excited women of the tribe. They were preparing the young girls for the ceremony that would initiate them into womanhood. All girls who had commenced their cycle of menstruation participated in this ancient ceremony.

The ritual of the dance was a platform to reintroduce the young girls to the tribe now as new, young women. Adetoun was not only very excited, but she felt a little extra pressure to perform the rituals correctly. As the Chief's daughter, she knew that many of the other girls would be looking to her as an example.

As the final touches were made to her hair, she was ready to dress. With great care, she slipped her arms into her ceremonial costume. Since birth, each of her aunties had lovingly contributed to the intricate artwork on her elaborate robe. Proudly stroking the material, Adetoun felt much loved and she blushed, as she knew that this would be the same robe in which she would be wed.

As the girls dressed for the ceremony, there was a great sense of anticipation in the air. The sacred days that were most celebrated by the tribe were births, deaths, marriages and the initiation ceremonies for manhood and womanhood.

Giggling amongst themselves, they knew also that the young men of the tribe would be looking even more closely at them. For after today, each one of the girls could be considered a prospective wife. With all the preparations completed and their headdresses carefully positioned, the girls nervously waited for the tribe to gather.

Peering out at the gathering crowd, Adetoun began looking at the young men of the tribe not as pesky boys, but as possible husbands. She thought to herself, "It is good to have a smart husband, so maybe Elewa would be best for me." Immediately, she thought that Elewa was a bit of a coward and might not be able to protect her very well. Sighing, she thought, "Perhaps then I should choose Naasir, as he is a proud warrior." Pondering on this for a moment, she then thought, "Hmmm, a strong warrior he may be, but he is very serious and does not laugh very much."

Confusing herself further, she then thought, "I want someone who is going to be sweet and soft like Jaafar. He always says such lovely things to me and makes me laugh." Adetoun's thoughts about her choice for a future husband were dispelled by the sounds of the ceremonial drums.

As the beating of the drums signaled the commencement of the ceremony, it also made the girls' hearts beat faster. This was their signal to walk out of the hut and proceed to the front of the gathering. As the girls slowly walked down the path, the women of the tribe threw fragrant flowers before them. As they arrived at the front of the tribe, the girls nervously assembled. They stood bunched up against each other; more so for emotional, rather than physical, support.

As the drums halted, the crowd parted and the Shaman of the tribe stepped forward. Reciting ancient African incantations and prayers, he waved his arms around each girl and sprinkled her with protective herbs and elixirs. Turning to face the large tribe, the Shaman spoke not only with authority, but with great concern and love in his voice.

He explained that after today, each young woman would be able to access the wisdom of certain African gods. This knowledge would help them along their new path as young women.

The Shaman told them about Elegua, the god of new beginnings. He explained that Elegua is the guardian of the crossroads of life and the girls were told to look to him for advice on what path would be best for them.

Next, the Shaman told the girls about Abassi. At the sound of this god's name, all the girls blushed and hid their faces. The Shaman told them what many of them already knew. Abassi was a creator god and he would help each one with their new sexual encounters.

Knowing that a wedded union is fraught with many adjustments, the Shaman gave the girls some marital advice. He told them that if arguments arose with their new husbands, not to pick up the nearest tree branch and beat their beloved over the head. His good-natured comments brought snickering and laughter from the crowd.

He gently suggested that the young women could instead seek the help of Eshu, as he is the god of communication.

They could also call upon Olorun, who is the god of peace and justice. The Shaman reminded the girls that wherever communication lives, justice and peace are sure to reside together. And lastly, the Shaman spoke about the god Yemaya. She was the mother of waters and helped women during childbirth.

As the drums started to rhythmically beat once more, the girls began to perform their well-rehearsed dance of womanhood. Concentrating very hard, Adetoun made sure that each step was perfect and elegant. The beautiful, expressive dance was both flowing and graceful. As the dance ended, the young ladies were relieved and proud of their performances.

Carrying a handful of beautiful colored necklaces, The Shaman asked each girl to kneel down as he said a prayer for them. He then carefully slipped a necklace over each of their heads. The faces of the tribe beamed with pride. Every tribe member had known the girls from birth and had been involved in the care, attention and love in raising them. Many had visible tears in their eyes on this momentous day.

As Adetoun knelt down, she closed her eyes and felt the Shaman put her necklace over her head.

Suddenly the air exploded with a crackling sound of thunder. Gazing up into a perfectly clear sky, the tribe members were confused as to what had made such a great sound. Watching in horror and disbelief, they saw their beloved Shaman fall to the ground as blood flowed freely from the gaping bullet wound in his chest.

Just then, more thunder was heard. Savage, snarling dogs came crashing through the forest, closely followed by a group of ghostly pale men in odd dress. These white English slave traders were carrying shiny sticks and waving large nets over their heads. The tribe, frozen in disbelief, had never seen white people before and their foreign English language sounded just like the barking of their dogs. As more thunder rang out from the barrel of their shotguns, one of the slave traders yelled out, "Stop shooting. Dead darkies won't increase our quota. Take them alive."

Although absolutely horrified at the advancing men and dogs, many of the tribe were so traumatized by this strange scene that they were riveted to the spot, unable to move. Others sensed that the same fate that befell their beloved Shaman was in store for them, and they scattered into the deep growth of the forest.

Paralyzed in shock and fear, Adetoun suddenly felt someone grab her arm. Looking up in horror, she was relieved to see that it was her Aunt Ngozi. Dragging Adetoun behind her, Ngozi's instincts told her to run deep into the safety of the forest.

As they fled the advancing white men, they felt the branches and twigs cutting deep into their skin. Numb to the pain of their torn flesh, their only concern was getting as much distance between them and the advancing strangers. Even though she felt the sting of the low hanging branches that whipped across her face, Ngozi was able to think clearly. She remembered a large, hollowed-out tree trunk down by the riverbank and thought that it would afford them a safe place to hide.

As the women burst through the forest and approached the river, they saw many of their loved ones running across the rocks of the shallow riverbed. Pulling Adetoun into the hollowed-out tree trunk,

Ngozi quickly broke off leaf-laden branches and hurriedly placed them at the opening. Clinging to each other in the semi-darkness, they froze in silence. The pounding of their hearts was drowned out by the terrified screams and cries of their friends and family.

Adetoun shuddered as she recognized some of the voices behind those screams. Jamming her fingers into her ears, she tried to shut out the cries of her cherished childhood friends. It was hard to believe that she and her friends had been giggling and performing together mere minutes ago. Pressed up against her Auntie's side for reassurance, Adetoun felt some comfort, as Ngozi was her favorite Aunt. Ngozi's name meant blessing and her beautiful nature was a blessing to everyone who knew her.

Listening to the wailing and anguished pleas of her people, Ngozi's heart stopped as she suddenly became aware of yet another sound. The barking of the dogs that had been heard in the distance now seemed to be advancing closer. She prayed to the gods that the dogs would pass the tree and not pick up their scent. Just as she had finished her prayers, two dogs burst into their hiding place and started to maul the women. Frantically kicking at the savage dogs, a huge hand appeared and grabbed at the dogs' collars. Yanking them out of the tree trunk, an ugly, hairy face poked through the entrance.

"Hallo, hallo, what do we have 'ere?"

Cringing in horror, the women recoiled at the sight of yellow, decaying teeth and a foul stench. The man's stinking sweat and accumulated layers of filth caused Adetoun to gag.

"Come on me lovelies, hide and seek is over. You lose!"

Grabbing each woman, he slipped a chain around their necks and dragged them from the tree trunk. As they gazed in horror, they saw family members lying crumpled on the ground. Many were dazed by the vicious beatings that halted their escape. Barely able to breathe, the bloody mass of tribe members was shackled together. Adetoun and Ngozi were the last to have their chains secured to the others.

The sound of thunder rang out once again from one of the shiny sticks.

"Okay, I'm only going to say this once. Get on your feet, move and don't stop moving until we tell you."

His words could just as well have fallen on deaf ears, as the tribe's members had no idea what he was saying. To help them translate quicker, the white men walked up and down the line beating the weary slaves, forcing them to their feet. Once they were standing, the shackled line of battered bodies started to move as one through the trampled forest.

The chained slave caravan slowly made its way to one of the several coastal ports of West Africa. Along the way, they were joined by similar groups of captured slaves from different tribes, all making their way in the same direction. Although Adetoun's captors were white, it was mainly African traders that transported slaves from the interior of Africa to the coastal ports.

Beaten and underfed, many captured Africans did not survive these death marches. Although barely alive like many of the others, Adetoun had the resilience of her youth. Her indignation and anger became etched in the form of a permanent scowl on her beautiful face.

After several months of marching through the forest, Ngozi noticed a different smell in the air and heard a strange sound of rhythmic crashing. Looking down at her swollen feet, she also noticed that the ground was gradually becoming reflective and lighter. As the forest became less dense, an amazing sight loomed before her. Having marched over a thousand miles from their village, they now stood in awe of an incredible view. There before them lay the Atlantic Ocean; a sight that was new to many of the tribes.

The lash of a whip against their flesh brought the caravan fully back into the moment.

"Move on, move on. You're holding up the line."

They were unaware that they had finally made it to one of the port towns that had become holding points for the slaves. Adetoun and her caravan were herded like cattle into underground dungeons.

These stone fortresses were used as holding pens for the slaves. One had to make sure that enough slaves were accumulated in order to fill a slave ship and make the journey economically viable. As her group was forced into the already crammed dungeon, Adetoun tried to adjust her eyes to the dark. As her eyes took in the writhing, bleeding heap of humanity, she shut her eyes and clung desperately close to her Aunt.

Although the wait for the slave ships to arrive could take up to one year, the ship they were destined to board docked within a month. Being allowed to resurface after being underground for so long, Adetoun was blinded as her eyes adjusted to being in the sunlight once again.

Shuffling as a group, the slaves were herded along and pushed to the ground. Adetoun watched off in the distance as hundreds of slaves filed onto a ship anchored off shore. She gasped as she realized that they were all naked. Just then, several African men in English dress approached her group.

Seeing their black skin, she whispered for them to quickly set them free so that they could escape into the forest. Answering her in some strange language, one of the men took out a large knife and held it against her ceremonial robe. In one swift action, he cut the robe off of Adetoun, leaving her young body naked and exposed. Mortified, she crouched down and tightly held her knees as her tears of shame stained her cheeks. She watched as a similar fate befell all the others in her group as they were stripped bare.

Although it was a tradition in their tribe that females were often bare breasted, it was unheard of for any adults in the tribe to openly expose themselves. Adetoun cringed as she saw the humiliation and deep shame reflected in other tribe members' faces.

It was then that one of the white slave traders came towards her group carrying a long metal pole with a red glow at the end. While several men grabbed one of the slaves and held him to the ground, another slave trader thrust the red hot branding iron with the ships initials onto the arm of the screaming man.

Adetoun was grabbed by the hair and held to the ground by a mud-encrusted boot on her neck. Paralyzed in fear as to what was happening, she howled in excruciating pain as the branding iron melted her skin and released the acrid smell of her burning flesh. This made life easier for the slave trader as there would be no mix-ups and no question as to who owned the slaves.

Half dead from the pain, the slaves then heard the crack of a whip over their heads. Adetoun's group slowly rose to their feet, shuffled towards the shoreline and loaded onto smaller boats. Looking at all the people making their way to the larger ship anchored in deeper waters, she wondered how many more the vessel could hold.

As her boat arrived at the large ship, her shackled group dragged themselves up the ramp. Adetoun looked over her shoulder and wept, not knowing when or if she would ever see her beautiful homeland again.

Descending into the bowels of the ship, the men and the women were separated. Adetoun had to bend over to maneuver into a crawl space that was barely three feet high. Along with the other slaves, she was forced to lie on her back with her head between another's legs, and then chained to the deck. Crammed together in these crawl spaces, devoid of light and air, Adetoun tried to block out the agonizing sound of wailing and moaning of the human cargo that echoed through the ship's hull.

Unfortunately for Adetoun, the captain was known for "tight packing" a ship. Because the slave trade was purely for profit, captains of vessels tried to deliver as many healthy slaves for as little cost as possible. Some captains used a system called "loose packing," transporting fewer slaves, which reduced sickness and death. Yet the captains who were known as "tight packers" believed that many slaves would not survive the Middle Passage crossing to America and were inclined to pack as many slaves as they could cram in.

The scorching midday sun increased the heat of the sweltering bodies and made the temperature in the hull of the ship inhumane. Unable to bear the heat, the tormented cries, and the unspeakable horror of being kidnapped, branded and enslaved, Adetoun thankfully fainted. In just a few months, this precious young girl and her people had been ripped from their homeland, lost their families and friends, and had their identity erased just because of the color of their skin.

For the next three months, Adetoun and the other 424 slaves would have to endure the most unspeakable degradation and violence.

Chained to the floor and made to lie down naked on the wooden planks, the constant rolling of the ship wore away large sections of their flesh. Stuffed and packed together in this manner, the slaves often lay in each other's feces, urine and blood. The stench was unbearable.

As a result, disease ran rampant throughout the ships with dysentery, yellow fever and small pox. It was not uncommon to awake and find that the person next to you had died during the night.

Periodically, the slaves were hauled up on deck in order to clean out the hold. Whipped and made to dance, they were exercised in order to keep them healthy. Adetoun watched in frozen horror as some slaves threw themselves overboard to escape the anguish and misery that they were forced to endure. It was preferable to be eaten by the sharks than to bear such a living hell.

Others tried to end the cruelty by not eating. As every slave filled a quota, the ship's crew had devised a sharp contraption that pried open the mouths of those who tried to starve themselves to death.

At the precious age of twelve, Adetoun had become numb, as she was made to watch constant beatings and the violent, brutal rape of the women on board. The only thing that kept her from throwing herself overboard was her deep attachment to her beloved Aunt. She clung to her dear Aunt Ngozi in order to maintain some sanity and human connection in an inhuman environment.

After ninety days, the ship pulled into the port of Fredericksburg, Virginia. The human cargo was purged from the ship and herded into holding pens. After months of the most unspeakable treatment possible, Adetoun watched in utter amazement, as the slaves were now compassionately attended to. They were shaved and their skins were oiled and polished. After months of total neglect, their festering sores were covered and dressed. Large servings of food were brought in and the slaves were encouraged to eat as much as they liked. Many slaves overate to such an extent that their starved, swollen bellies rejected the food.

The slaves were then made to dress in white man's clothing.

Adetoun was forced to wear a long dress and scratchy undergarments. The rough fabric felt foreign against her body after being naked for so many months. Along with the other women, she practiced taking long, slow strides, so as not to get caught up in the material and trip over with every step.

A booming voice stopped the women in their tracks as a huge white man appeared with a stick. Pushing and prodding the women, they were forced forward to the front of the holding pen.

A large sheet that was covering the front of the pen was pulled aside to reveal men and women who had come to bid at the slave auction. This inspection period was held before the auction to enable the bidders to examine "the goods." In this way, the bidders made sure that they were getting value for their money.

Adetoun cringed as she saw the white people pulling open the mouths of the slaves to check their teeth while they pinched and poked their skin. Many of the slaves were forced to dance, in order to show the intended buyer how flexible and agile they were. As the viewing period came to an end, the sheet was pulled across once more. Unable to see, Adetoun listened as the gathered crowd of bidders grew quiet.

She then heard only one man's voice. The auctioneer was jovial and he enthusiastically welcomed everyone. Hoping to excite the crowd into a buying frenzy, he told them that this was the finest stock that had ever been auctioned and it was one of the largest hauls to cross the Atlantic.

Quickly presenting the rules and going over the bill of sale information, he said that they had better get started as they had a full day ahead of them. Announcing that the bucks would be sold first, Adetoun watched as all the men were herded out of the pen and taken out of sight. Not knowing what was going to happen next, she clung close to her Aunt's side.

Beyond sight of the slave auction, the women could not see what was going on, but they could hear shouting and yelling. For hours, the women were made to wait in the sweltering temperatures. Overheated in her new dress and stifled by the humidity of a typical Virginia summer's afternoon, Adetoun had lay on the ground and drifted off to sleep.

The sound of several men bursting into the holding pen and pushing the women startled her awake. Quickly running to catch up with her Aunt, Adetoun and the other women were herded into a huge square. She saw a sea of people surrounding a central figure standing on a platform next to a tall, raised cement block. One by one, the women were forced to stand on the block in full view of the crowd.

According to the age and condition of the slave, the auctioneer set a price and let the bidding begin. With each woman who was sold, Adetoun's group dwindled in size. Suddenly, Aunt Ngozi was grabbed and put on show. Naturally, not wishing to be separated from her Aunt, Adetoun followed her. Out of nowhere, a huge blow to her stomach knocked the wind out of Adetoun and sent her sprawling to the ground. "See, they are so excited that they just can't wait to be sold!" The crowd roared with laughter at the auctioneer's joke.

A wealthy plantation owner from North Carolina needed more field hands and was buying up big. He won the bid for Aunt Ngozi, who was lead to a cart to join his other purchases.

Desperately wanting to go with her Aunt, Adetoun ran into the open square and hopped on to the block. This brought squeals of laughter from the crowd. As the bidding started, Adetoun's eyes were drawn to a lady carrying a pink parasol. She was so white that her skin resembled the underbelly of a toad. Her arm was intertwined with that of an older man sporting a full beard and a moustache. Adetoun thought that he looked like a goat. The lady kept pointing to Adetoun and whispering in the man's ear.

As the hammer fell with the closing bid, Adetoun was now the property of the sickly-looking lady and her husband. Jumping to the ground, Adetoun started to run towards Aunt Ngozi's cart.

A black man with a rope approached her and firmly grabbed her arm. "Now dat ain't no way to start, after Massa and Missus Randolph done paid good money for you. Now come on over here to our cart and we'll get you settled for the long ride home."

Although this man's manner seemed to be kind and caring, Adetoun didn't understand a single word that he was saying. Held fast in his strong grasp, a panic swept over Adetoun as she craned her neck to keep her beloved Aunt in sight. Her face lit up as she saw her Aunt in one of the overcrowded carts. But just then, Aunt Ngozi's cart started to pull away from the square and Adetoun started to yell and fight to free herself.

"What ya'll doin, Missy? Don't be like that or I'll have to get this here whip to you quick smart, even before ya get to the plantation." Adetoun froze in confusion, not understanding a word he said. He cracked the whip above her head to make his point, frightening Adetoun as she bit her lip in fear, drawing blood.

Desperately crying and beating her head, Adetoun watched her beloved Aunt roll out of her life forever. Sobbing uncontrollably, Adetoun was dragged, tied up and crammed into a cart full of slaves. Heaving loudly, she had no way of knowing that she was journeying to the birth of her new life. Yet, with the loss of her beloved Aunt, a part of Adetoun had died.

Adetoun's new owners, the Randolph family, owned a tobacco plantation near Charlottesville, Virginia. This huge sprawling property was one of the largest in the area and had over one hundred slaves. The journey from Fredericksburg, in the crammed, bumpy cart was barely noticed by Adetoun as she was traumatized having been separated from her beloved Aunt.

After many hours, the cart turned off the main road and Adetoun saw two massive stone pillars and a long tree-lined driveway. As the cart rolled along, she noticed many slaves working in the fields. Rounding a bend in the road, Adetoun could not believe her eyes.

The four-story Georgian house that appeared before her was home to William Harrison Randolph and Adella Randolph and their six children. As slave carts were not permitted in the front driveway, it slowly veered off a side road that wound its way along the woods.

Coming over the crest of a hill, Adetoun saw the slave cabins that were perched on the verge of the forest. The clever placement of these cabins was well thought out; as they were in close proximity to the great manor house. In this way, the slaves were not only readily accessible to their owners, they could always see the manor house looming before them as a symbol of dominance.

As soon as the cart stopped, a black woman came over and started to speak in a loud, shrill voice. "Would ya just looky here at this sad and sorry lot." Walking around the cart, she screwed up her nose and said, "Here I goes agin. Just as soon as I's teach these dumb Africans what to do and set them straight, then another cartload comes right along."

Her name was Sally Randolph and like many of the slaves, she had been born on the plantation. At seventeen years of age, all she had ever known was a life of bondage and being controlled. She liked being in authority and controlling others.

With the slaves not understanding English, Sally waved her arms frantically about to convey to them to get out of the cart. Sally's actions reminded Adetoun so much of a squawking chicken that she started to laugh. Grabbing Adetoun by the hair, Sally thought to make an example of her disobedience. Dragging Adetoun out of the cart, she threw her in the dirt. This was Adetoun's introduction to the definite pecking order that was to be strictly followed in order to survive.

That evening, Adetoun felt the sting of the scrapes on her legs as she lay on a bed of straw. She closed her eyes tightly and tried to replace the pain with the memories of her family and homeland. To help her, she tried to remember the Shaman's words of wisdom that he had shared at her womanhood ceremony.

In her most reverent voice, she silently whispered prayers to Olorun, the god of peace and justice, to help her captors find it in their hearts to let her return home. She didn't pray for long, as she fell into a deep, exhaustive sleep.

A quick jab in her side startled her awake at 5:00a.m. Squinting through sleepy eyes, Adetoun saw the first sliver of dawn's light appear on the horizon. Still rubbing sleep from her eyes, she was taken up to the main house and told to wait by the back door.

Adetoun was startled as the door flew open and a large lady with a round, kind face stood in the doorway.

"Now let's have a good look at you. Missus said you were sure enough pretty. But, I sure do hopes you have enough sense in that curly head of yours to keep ye sef out of trouble."

Kizzy had been cook for the Randolphs for many years and, although it was not official, she ran the household staff.

"Pretty you may be, but you sure is skinny. Come on child, ifn we gonna get a decent day's work out of ya, then you gotta be fed."

As she watched Adetoun devour her food, Kizzy pointed to herself, and said, "Kizzy, I is Kizzy."

Putting her hand gently on Adetoun's shoulder, she then pointed to Adetoun and asked, "What's yo name?"

For the first time in almost five months, someone had shown her some tenderness. As tears started to form in her big, brown eyes and stream down her cheeks, she pointed to herself and in a shaky voice said, "Adetoun."

Kizzy then shook her head and quickly said, "Massa don't like no African names in this house."

Taking off her apron, Kizzy wiped away Adetoun's tears and said in a soft tone, "Now hush, child. You stay close to me and learn and you'll be all right."

Later on that morning, a bell rang in the kitchen and summoned Kizzy to bring the Missus her breakfast in bed. Pregnant with her seventh child, Adella Randolph was always feeling poorly and spent a great deal of time in bed these days. Following closely behind Kizzy, Adetoun stood silently in the doorway. As Kizzy set down the breakfast tray and pulled open the curtains, she helped the Missus to sit up and propped pillows behind her back.

Setting her eyes upon Adetoun, Adella said, "Kizzy, I pray, do tell me who we have here?"

Kizzy replied, "Ma'am, she is the new girl you wanted for the house."

Waving her arms, Adella motioned for the girl to come closer to her bed. As Adetoun slowly walked up to Mrs. Randolph's bedside, the strong, sweet smell of rose water and lavender made her feel queasy. Adella took hold of Adetoun's face as if examining an object. "What is her name?"

"Her name done be Adetoun."

Adella was horrified. "Now, Kizzy, we can't have a slave with a name that sounds so much like mine; just think of all the confusion." Furrowing her brow beneath her white bonnet, Adella spent several moments in deep thought. She then proudly announced, "I know, Kizzy. We will call her Eliza; that is a much better name for her now."

Pleased as punch with her name selection, Adella turned her attention to her breakfast, waved her hand and dismissed them both.

As Eliza Randolph shuffled down the steps after Kizzy, she did not realize it, but today was her thirteenth birthday. And the only present she had been given was a new name.

In the months that followed, Eliza would come to envy the slaves working in the fields. Their workdays were clearly sunrise to sunset. But the life of a household slave was never-ending. She was expected to cook, clean, serve meals, look after children, wash, iron, weed the garden and collect eggs and firewood. In addition, once the fruits and vegetables were harvested, she had to preserve them, filling up the larders for the long, harsh winters to come. It was expected of a house slave to also weave, quilt and spin linens.

Adella Randolph was a very religious woman and loved to read Bible verses to the slaves. She drummed it into Eliza's head that she was a sinner and that idle hands were the devil's playground. And, while Eliza kept herself busy as she did not want the devil to get her, she feared for Adella as she never saw anyone who was more idle and lazy than her Missus.

Eliza slept on a pallet in an alcove in the hallway, right next to the bedrooms. In this way, she was on call during the night to tend the sick or fetch food, wood, water or empty chamber pots for the members of the household. Eliza knew that although her work seemed endless, she was fortunate in one way. She saw the cruelty that was inflicted by the overseer on the field hands. Many times the slaves would be gathered to watch the punishment of a disobedient or runaway slave. Beating, dismembering and castrating slaves was deemed legal and seen as a necessary course of action to ensure the safety of one's property. In this way, the slaves had a constant reminder of who was in control and that they had no freedom at all.

During the months that followed, Eliza's once clear, bright eyes had taken on an empty, hollow look of resignation. Knowing full well that she was the new slave in the house, she kept pretty much to herself. Kizzy was the only person she felt comfortable with and she looked forward to being with her. In the beginning, she had helped Kizzy prepare dinners, clean and iron. But as Adella's pregnancy advanced, Eliza's time was spent attending more and more to the needs of the Missus.

And although each day seemed to be never-ending, this past week was worse than ever. Massa Randolph was entertaining some prominent businessmen and the nights were filled with lavish dinners and heavy drinking. On top of the added food preparation and cleaning, Eliza had spent a grueling day running up and down the long, winding staircase, fetching and attending to Adella's every whim. Finally, late at night, Eliza collapsed onto her pallet in the alcove.

As she was just about to drift off to sleep, a single candle illuminated the darkness at the end of the corridor. Eliza froze as she watched the intoxicated, hulking figure of Massa Randolph advance down the hallway. The sickly smell of alcohol preceded him as he entered Adella's bedroom. As a result of her pregnancy and ailing health, the couple had taken to sleeping in different rooms. A few moments later, Eliza could hear muffled voices and Adella calling him an animal and yelling for him to get away from her in her condition.

Suddenly, the door of Adella's bedroom burst open and a stark naked Massa appeared, clothes and candle in hand. Eliza gasped loudly at this strange sight. Noticing the sound, Massa Randolph thrust the candle into the dark alcove. As Eliza's face came into the light, he began to laugh. Dropping his clothes, he reached into the alcove and grabbed Eliza. Drunkenly stumbling down the hallway, with one hand gripped onto Eliza and the other hand carrying the candle, he burst into his bedroom and threw Eliza on the bed. Putting the candle down, he turned the key in the lock. Staggering back and forth, he saw the open window and tossed the key through it. Frightened and trembling, Eliza watched him advance towards her. His huge, naked body fell upon her and he started to rub her breasts and grope between her legs. Eliza began to scream, but the Massa quickly covered her month and started to mount her.

With all her strength and all the defiance, anger and fury that had accumulated since she was ripped from her homeland, she opened her mouth and bit down as hard as she could. As her teeth sank into his flesh, he let go and cried out in pain. Sneering in disbelief, he picked Eliza up by the neck and punched her in the head. The brutal force of the blow split the side of her face and sent Eliza flying into the wall; shattering her skull. Massa Randolph threw himself onto her crumpled form, tightened one hand around her neck and penetrated her dying body.

Eliza looked behind the Massa, and there stood the Shaman of her tribe. With great joy in her voice, she cried out, "You've come to rescue me. Please take me home!"

Taking the Shaman's outstretched hand, she gently rose above her body. As they walked into the tunnel, Eliza looked back over her shoulder and saw the Massa raping the young girl's lifeless body.

9

Heaven – Our Angelic Support

Ever since she had been torn from her family and African home, Eliza had shut down her glorious light. In order to endure the endless cruelty and violence, she had forced herself to become numb and emotionally dead. The Shaman knew where to take Eliza; as this kind of trauma needed long-term attention. Arriving at the Spirit Hospital, loving angels were ready to take care of her. As they tenderly wrapped and cocooned her in a sleep-induced state, Eliza fell into the first peaceful sleep that she had known since her capture.

Her deep emotional pain took a great length of time to heal. With the constant care and attention from the angels, she slowly regained her health, allowing the precious light inside of her to radiate once more. Over time, her increased vibrations and light alerted the Shaman that her health had finally been restored. Walking into the Spirit Hospital, the Shaman saw Eliza deep in contemplation as she sat by a nearby fountain.

A low, booming voice shook Eliza out of her reflection. "I've got a present for you."

Recognizing the familiar voice, Eliza ran towards the Shaman and threw her arms around him. An immense feeling of gratitude welled in her heart and her voice trembled. "Thank you so much for rescuing me."

As a huge smile spread over his face, the Shaman reached behind his back and presented her with some folded cloth. "It has been waiting for you to get well."

Eliza's face lit up as she unfolded it, revealing the designs of her ceremonial robe. Joyful tears tumbled down her smiling face. Moving very slowly, as if she didn't want to wake herself from a beautiful dream, she gently put her arms into the sleeves and let the robe fall around her body.

"We were so rudely interrupted during your ceremony," said the Shaman. Opening his hand, the necklace from that day appeared. Placing it over Eliza's head, the Shaman looked down at her and beamed with pride. "Young women who perform well have more than earned their celebration party." Holding out his arm to her, he announced, "Come Adetoun, the tribe is waiting for you."

Having been trained to answer to her slave name Eliza, Adetoun beamed with pride on hearing her true, tribal name. Taking the Shaman's arm, they walked out of the Spirit Hospital and stared in wonder as the forest of her African homeland rapidly appeared before them. Adetoun stepped onto the familiar ground cover and inhaled the reassuring scents of the forest in which she had grown up.

As they walked deeper into the forest, the air was suddenly filled with voices and a large gathering of people appeared. Approaching the gathering, Adetoun recognized familiar faces from the tribe and the cherished group of girls who were so dear to her. In unison they gleefully cried, "Come on, come, Adetoun. We've waited for you to start the celebrations." Running towards them, they embraced, as they were finally together again.

As part of the celebration, a treasured loved one would take turns telling an endearing story from the lives of each one of the young ladies. When Adetoun's turn came, she walked over to the seat of honor, sat down and waited patiently.

Out of nowhere, a voice started to speak.

"Although I remember everything about my lovely Adetoun, I experienced her true beauty and splendor under the most devastating conditions. Adetoun, you thought that it was I keeping you alive. But with your strength of character and tremendous courage, you made me stronger and kept me choosing life. I love you deeply."

As the crowd parted, Adetoun's cherished Aunt Ngozi stepped forward. As she looked upon her precious Aunt again, tears of immense joy streamed down Adetoun's cheeks. In sheer elation, they ran towards each other and embraced. In that one embrace, all the longing, all the grief, all the devastation that they had experienced together spilled forth and was healed. As the angels looked on, they wept, for they couldn't remember a more loving, joyous and triumphant homecoming party.

Sensing that the time had come to leave, the Shaman approached Adetoun. Taking her hand, he told her that they had to go to another ceremony. Sensing her apprehension of being separated from her tribe once again, he assured her that she could revisit her cherished tribe whenever she desired. Trusting her beloved Shaman, they proceeded to walk through her familiar forest. They had not walked far when Adetoun began to notice that the forest was becoming less dense and that more flowers were appearing along the path.

As an overwhelming scent of beautiful flowers filled the air, the immense towering Hall of Justice appeared before her. The Shaman explained that this is where a review of her life would take place and that she would be well protected. Taking off his lion's tooth necklace, he placed it around her throat and laid it upon her chest.

"Have courage, Adetoun. I will be waiting for you when your review is complete."

Walking up the massive stone steps of the building, Adetoun entered the room and sat down on the bench. As the holographic images appeared, she watched each moment of her precious life unfold before her.

While watching the images of her life as a captured slave, she grabbed the lion's tooth necklace with such force that the tooth embedded a deep imprint into the palm of her hand. As she reviewed that fateful night when Mr. Randolph killed her, she felt the loving arms of the angels surrounding her and letting her know that she was protected from any further harm.

Having completed her review, Adetoun stepped out into the glorious sunlight and felt the warmth on her face. As promised, the Shaman was waiting for her. As she was led to the Hall of Akashic Records, Adetoun's mood was contemplative and reflective. Walking up the marble steps, she felt a familiar sense that she had been here before. Upon entering the grand Hall, she approached the semi-circle of the Etheric Council awaiting her arrival.

"Welcome Home, Ariel. It is a pleasure to see you once again."

On hearing her real name, Ariel started to remember that this was her one true Home. "It is good to be Home once again," she said with a tender smile.

With much concern, the Elders opened up her Book of Life. "You know, you had us worried for a while there, precious one. You had to be cocooned for quite some time before your vibrations returned to their bright radiance once again." Looking at her contract, the Council asked her, "Tell us about the life that you just lived."

Ariel drew a deep breath before answering. "Having treated others with disregard in my former life of wealth and privilege, I wanted to learn what it felt like to be oppressed and to be treated in the same manner. In my life as a slave, I was able to experience what it feels like to have all my freedoms denied and every shred of my identity stripped away."

The Council listened intently. "What did you learn from this life?"

Ariel slowly replied, "This life was probably the most important of all my lives thus far. It taught me that even though I was stripped of my possessions, my homeland, my family and my freedoms, my captors could not destroy my soul. I was able to keep my dignity, love and my deep faith alive in my heart. I guess the only way we can truly see our glorious connection to God is to have everything stripped away from us. Only when a soul is completely bare, can we see it as a Divine reflection of God."

The Etheric Council sat quietly in awe as they witnessed an enormous opening on Ariel's path of spiritual enlightenment. "My dear Ariel, this wise awareness that you have so eloquently expressed has pleased us more than you can know. For under horrific circumstances, you kept your light of God alive. You are thanked and more profoundly loved than you can possibly imagine."

Each member of the Council then stood, bowed and acknowledged Ariel. Signing and sealing her contract, they closed her Book of Life.

Walking out of the beautiful Hall, Ariel felt very different than she had after her other incarnations. Previously, after returning from Earth, she felt as if she needed time to escape to rebuild her depleted energies. Yet, with her newly acquired spiritual awareness, her vibrations dramatically increased. Instead of wanting to rest, she hungered to learn more. This immense yearning for more information immediately manifested a place of higher learning.

Ariel's thoughts instantly transported her to an outdoor amphitheater. Decorative stone columns surrounded the immense circular structure, which was set in a lush, verdant garden. Walking into the arena, the seats were filled with eager souls who were anxiously waiting for the presentation to begin. Just like Ariel, the other souls were ready to take the next step along the journey of their spiritual enlightenment. As soon as she sat down, a hush fell over the assembled group.

Looking toward the stage, the audience heard a powerful, yet comforting voice and watched a deep blue light merge into form.

"Hello my name is Archangel Metatron. Unlike most of the other Archangels, and just like you, I have also lived a life as a human before becoming an Archangel. Knowing what it means to transcend the cycle of physical life, I help people with spiritual knowledge as they advance on their path of enlightenment. As God's scribe, I record this important spiritual wisdom in the Hall of Akashic Records."

Lovingly gazing out at the sea of expectant faces in the amphitheater, Archangel Metatron continued, "I would like to congratulate each one of you, for you have chosen to see your incarnation from a higher perspective. In so doing you have walked through a remarkable door that leads to a path of awakened awareness. Viewing our lives from a higher perspective, one clearly starts to see our incarnations, not as separate events, but as an extraordinary tapestry of experiences. It is in the weaving of this conscious awareness and perception that we begin to build a foundation of spiritual knowledge.

"Each one of you is a special energy with unique gifts and talents. Yet, at the same time, you are also a part of a mass collective consciousness. Take this knowing and realize that each of the Archangels that will be presented to you is no greater than you are. They have chosen to realize their Divine eternal nature and connectedness to God in their every waking moment. And so it is."

As Metatron's deep blue light began to fade, a bright yellow light enfolded and bathed the stage with its glow. Out of that yellow light stepped a form.

"Hello, my name is Archangel Uriel and I will be your first Teacher. We here in Heaven watch as many souls are on an eternal quest to reach spiritual enlightenment. Yet, true progress on their path may only be made when one securely grounds ones spiritual knowledge in physical reality. This is what it means to live Heaven on Earth."

Archangel Uriel's light began to glow brighter. Leaning toward the audience, he lowered his voice. "I'll let you all in on a secret. Many souls want to go to Earth to become a part of this beautiful experience called ascension. And they incarnate in the physical even though they know that the journey will be challenging. But remember, no soul enters the Earth plane without already having all the ancient wisdom inside of them in order to face any challenges."

A lantern and a book appeared in his hands. "The lantern that I carry is a symbol of God's light shining on all of us," he explained. "And this book contains God's ordained laws that help us to make order out of our lives. As each of us already possesses this Divine knowledge in our soul, open up and bring forth your ancient wisdom."

He then held up the lantern and said, "May you always go in God's light."

And with those words, the yellow light began to recede. Yet, just as Archangel Uriel's light was dimming, a soft, green light became evident. As it started to intensify and fill the entire stage, Ariel noted how calm and serene she felt. As the light began to take form, Archangel Raphael stepped forward.

"Greetings, Beloved Ones. The reason so many of you are feeling as if a blanket of serenity has just covered you is that my comfort provides a nourishment that heals and helps souls return to a feeling of completeness. I have no magic power, for I have the same God-given ability as you have. To help bring you to that place of wholeness and peace, focus your attention on acknowledging the beauty and perfection of Mother Earth. By taking time to be with and connect with her spirit, you will allow peace and tranquility to surround you.

"The green of Mother Earth means renewal and shows us the perpetual cycle of life. Let her cleanse and transform that which does not serve you. In this way, you will start to achieve harmony once more. It is in the understanding of our illness and pain that we can reverse it. Perhaps our illness has shown us that we have strayed from our life plan or that we are dishonoring ourselves in a particular area. Because an illness is a mere symptom of being separate from God, the knowledge that we acquire from our illness may be used to assist in showing us the path back to unity with Divine Source. And it is so."

As the nourishing green light started to diminish, Ariel felt a shift within her physical body. This enormous wave of vibrations began to move to her heart and spread love throughout her entire being. The stage was suddenly covered in a soft, delicate shade of pink as petals fell softly on those seated in the amphitheater. The sweet smell of roses gently caught the air, and everyone's attention centered on the form emanating from the pink light.

"It is so lovely to be together once more. I am Archangel Chamuel and my name means 'he who seeks God.' I will help you strengthen your gifts of understanding, compassion and empathy. By teaching you to trust and to connect with your own Divine source inside, you become empowered to love yourselves. In this way, you can connect with others with compassion and understanding, to truly open your eyes in order to see the Divine within everyone. By exemplifying a life of unconditional love, we understand that we are all one. This feeling of unity and connectedness aligns us with the greatest force in the Universe and heals our separation from God.

"If only you could see yourself as God sees you. You are one of His children and He watches over you and protects you more than you can imagine. Hold this knowing of His profound love deep in your heart every second of the day. Feel His love surrounding you as if a great pink cloud envelops you. In being blessed with the gifts of free will and free choice, you have the power to choose love in all your decisions. By choosing love, you acknowledge your own Divinity and your holy light inside. Know with all your being that you are loved and held close to God's heart in every second. And so it is."

As the soft pink light started to fade, white wisps of clouds began to appear and float onto the stage. Mingled among the clouds was a beautiful sky blue color. Ariel felt as if she were weightless, drifting on these clouds, as a form appeared and Archangel Gabriel stepped forward.

"Salutations to all gathered here. I am Archangel Gabriel. As a messenger, I often bring news of new beginnings and renewals in your life. In this way, I help awaken you to your life's purpose. The more you acknowledge your gifts and talents and follow your heart, the more your journey in life will be nourishing. Remember that whatever you choose to do in life is not as important as how you choose to do it. By doing everything with a pure and loving heart, you will always emanate a glorious light. I will help support your intuitive messages, give you strength to believe in yourself, and encourage you to keep advancing forward.

"Through my gifts as a messenger, I will give you glimpses into your future by presenting dreams, signs and synchronicities so that you know which direction to take. Remember that all my messages are positive and filled with hope. You may faintly hear me whisper in your ear as a reminder to be joyful, grateful and to appreciate life. After all, our natural state is one of bliss. It is in this state of laughter and pure joy, that you will be closest to your true Divine self. I am always here for you. And it is so."

With the utterance of his last words, the colors started to change on stage. Ariel watched as the light blue turned to royal blue, then to navy, and finally became a deep indigo. Out of this color, two silvery forms began to emerge. As the edges became defined, everyone could discern that one was a shield and the other was a sword. Taking form in the middle was Archangel Michael. Stepping forward, he grasped his hands around the sword and the shield.

"Each and every one of you has the Divine ability to harness and use the powerful potential that is your birthright. Yet, when you doubt yourself and veer off the path of Divine truth, I, Archangel Michael, will help with clarifying, protecting and strengthening your faith in yourself. Put your desires into action. But always see to it, that it is done with faith and love. My sword symbolizes the extraordinary power of love that severs our attachments to things that do not serve us. When you are fearful and doubting yourself, I will help you understand the battle between dark and light. Allow my deep blue color to be a shield when you need protection from your doubts and fears. As we strengthen and connect to our personal power, we feel more self-assured and stronger. It is through our renewed strength, that we can exercise our capacity to be gentle and loving contributors to humanity.

"Another symbol representative of my energies is the scales of justice. Call on me to help you stand up for yourself and fight for what you believe to be right. In this way, you will stand up for your truth. Remember that your truth is not something that you have been told or brought up to believe in your childhood. You were born with these beliefs, it is not something that can be learned or taught to you by others. Your truth is a deep knowing in the profound depths of your heart and will only be revealed by looking within. We all have fears. Yet, it is in stepping forth in spite of our fears that will make you the strong warrior that we know that you are. Always live your Truth. And so it is."

With those words, the colors began to fade away, the stage went dark and the souls began to clear the amphitheater. Ariel sat for a long time contemplating all the wisdom that the Archangels had shared with the audience. As she sat in reflection, a great urgency began to build within her. As if awakened from a long sleep, this urgency found her propelled back on the path to the Hall of Akashic Records. Bursting through the doors with enthusiastic fervor, Ariel startled the Council.

Unable to contain her passion, she blurted out, "I've got to go back immediately. There was so much I missed by not being fully awakened. Please, beloved Elders, allow me to return without taking time to reflect on my past incarnation."

The Etheric Council was silent and their faces glowed with smiles of deep wisdom. They had heard this countless times before from impassioned souls who, having awoken to their inner wisdom, felt like they needed to go back immediately in order to 'get it right this time,' or 'fix it,' as if their last incarnations were somehow broken. Noting her enthusiasm and sensing the overwhelming passion in her heart, the Council kindly replied, "For one who is so rich in desiring to utilize and convey her spiritual knowledge to others, we happily grant you peace to return to the Earth plane whenever you want."

Reopening her Book of Life, Ariel contracted with the Elders the life's lessons and experiences that she would encounter on her next incarnation to Earth. The Council signed her contract and reminded her, "Ariel, go forth and be the reflection of God's Divine ancient wisdom. In this way, you will help others to access their own wisdom."

Letting the Council's kind words settle in her heart, Ariel thanked them and hurried excitedly out of the Hall.

Stepping onto the massive stone steps, Ariel knew that before she would return to Earth, she wanted to reconnect with some special loved ones. She became aware that the warmth of the sun seemed brighter, the colors of the flowers seemed more intense and the air smelled sweeter. She heard a soft, gentle voice nearby. "God's gifts are how they always were; it is only you who has now changed." Materializing in front of her was her beloved Twin Flame, Kiel.

Enfolding in each others' arms was truly coming Home. "I know we only have a short time together as you are eager to quickly go back and be of service," Kiel said. Knowing full well what her answer would be, he suggested, "Shall we take a walk together before you depart?"

As Ariel nodded, they instantly found themselves standing on the powdery white sand of their beloved beach. Their beautiful Victorian home could be seen in the distance. As they walked hand-in-hand, Ariel breathed deeply and noticed the familiar smell of the kelp and seaweed. The Twin Flames reconnected as they listened to the squawking seagulls and the rhythmic pounding of the waves against the shoreline.

As Ariel gazed at the beautiful stretch of beach, a little dot appeared in the distance and was followed by yips of delight. Running as fast as her little legs could carry her, Cleo wasn't going to be left out of this reunion party. Finally reaching Ariel, she leapt through the air into her arms and bathed her face in dog kisses. As they walked, Ariel and Kiel discussed their experiences and lessons learned in their incarnations on Earth.

As they sat in the dunes, Cleo chased the disappointed sand crabs that were hoping to come out for a quiet evening feed. Ariel looked lovingly at Kiel and said, "I dearly love our time together, but this time is somehow very different. I am being called back to serve in a greater capacity."

Knowingly, Kiel replied, "It is probably because you are going back with an awakened sense of spiritual knowledge." He held her hands and kissed her on the forehead. "Go, my beautiful Princess, and know that we will be right here for you anytime."

Looking into his love-filled eyes, Ariel's smiling face began to fade. And once again she found herself standing on the platform of the transition level. Although free from actual suitcases, she felt as if she was traveling back with precious cargo filled with spiritual knowledge to share with others. On hearing her name, Ariel tingled with anticipation as she stepped off the platform and into the tunnel once more.

10

North Dakota, America, 1810

As they made their way through the celebrations, the appearance of the eighteen-year-old twin brothers silenced the drums and halted the fire twirlers and dancers. As the crowd of Lakota parted for the young men, the crescendo of tribal chanting tapered off to a reverent hush. The twins' loving parents, Wambleesha and Zonta, looked on in great anticipation. It was difficult for either of them to recall a time when their sons were not in competition.

Tonight would be the culmination of their sons' trials and tests over the past ten years. As the old Medicine Man of the tribe, Wachinksapa, watched the boys approach, he could barely discern their features. With his advancing age, his eyesight had been steadily failing him over the past year. Poor vision and declining health had hastened the urgency for him to pass the 'magic' onto the next generation.

Zonta's heart was very heavy. She knew that this day would bring great honor and respect to one of her boys. Yet, the other son would have to endure a lifetime of knowing that he was only second best. Sensing the pain in her heart, Wambleesha put his strong arm around his wife as she wept silent tears. Zonta's ability to connect deeply with and intuit the feelings of all around her was reflected in her name, which meant 'Spirit.'

It seemed like only yesterday that Zonta found out that she had conceived. Almost immediately, she began to isolate herself and spent more time away from the tribe. This self-imposed isolation gave her greater opportunities to honor herself and the new life growing inside her. During her long walks through the forest, she would breathe deeply and quietly observe the gentle rhythms of life. Intuitively she knew that it was her attitude and respect for nature that would silently convey to her unborn child her reverence and connection to all creation. Her reverence for the miracle inside her was increased as she discovered mid-term that she had been blessed with carrying two babies.

During Zonta's nine months of pregnancy, the magnificent beauty of Mother Earth surrounded her. Zonta's delicate frame had trouble competing with the heavy weight of the twins. As the months passed, her long walks in nature had become less frequent and all she longed for was to lie down and rest. But the wise women of the tribe knew that regular walking would bring about a quicker and easier labor.

As Zonta's belly grew heavier with each passing day, the world around her seemed to grow lighter. The warm spring days encouraged the blossoming of new buds on the trees, and bright wild flowers burst forth, painting the fields. After such a long, colorless winter, it seemed like Mother Nature was in a hurry to decorate the Earth.

This glorious spring morning found the crones, the wise women of the tribe, visiting Zonta's tent. The group of women gently, yet firmly, persuaded her to help them collect wild flowers and berries. Zonta eagerly agreed to a walk, as Mother Nature's rebirth of spring beckoned her out of the tent. As they sat in the cool, tender shoots of the new spring grasses, the women chatted and shared their wisdom and life's experiences. Zonta felt fortunate to have so many 'Aunties' looking after her. As the shadows of the late afternoon started to lengthen, the group began to head back to their tents. As Zonta moved slowly back to camp, she could see her husband waving to her in the distance.

Zonta suddenly became aware of a trickle of water running down her leg. The women knew immediately that her water had broken and that labor was not far away. They excitedly called out to Wambleesha and he ran over to them, lifted Zonta up in his arms and carried her into their tent. As the group of women gathered around, Zonta's pain slowly started to increase.

The loving group of wise crones sat in the tent with her and carefully watched the signs of her labor. Having all assisted in many births, the older women were quick to pick up the unusually short spaces of time between contractions. Wave after wave of excruciating pain left Zonta breathless. One of the crones stated that it was more like a race to the finish than a birth. Just when she thought that the pain was too unbearable to endure, the head of the first baby started to crown.

One of the women said, "I wonder who will be the winner?"

As the baby's head appeared and then his body easily slipped into the world, the women drew breaths in amazement. There, firmly attached to the first baby's leg, was the little hand of his brother, as if trying to hold him back from coming first into the world. As the second twin was safely delivered, Zonta named her first-born Ohiyesa, which means 'winner.' She named her second born Akechta, which means 'fighter.' Little did Zonta realize how prophetic the choices of these names would become in the lives of her twin sons.

After giving birth, the first thing that Zonta did was to thank her sons for choosing her to be their mother. The tribe believed that all children chose their parents before birth. This powerful belief contributed to parents feeling blessed to have had this special spiritual being come into their lives. In the Lakota tribe, all children were considered sacred. They were honored from an early age as to their understanding of the spiritual laws of nature and the members of the tribe demonstrated love and special care to all the children. Even the Lakota word for children, 'waken,' means sacred.

From the moment of their birth and as they grew, no two boys were ever loved so much. The wise women had showed Zonta the great importance that the mother plays in the first two years of a child's life. Like all mothers, she was entrusted with the highest honor to instill in her children the connectivity and gifts of Mother Earth.

She would rise early in the morning, dress and feed her little charges, and set off for the day. She hummed softly to them as they walked the open field to reach the forest's edge. The canopy of trees offered an abundant classroom filled with wonders and magic. They were surrounded by birds that live closest to the Great Spirit, by the steadfast majestic trees, and by the cascading waters that sang the praises of Mother Earth. With this constant attention and devotion to nature, her children were brought up in absolute love, reverence and silence.

As the boys reached the milestone of their second birthday, Zonta's family started to play an increasing role in the upbringing of the boys. Having had the strong foundation of maternal bonding for the first two years, they were now ready to absorb the wisdom from other family members. Lakota wisdom knew that, although a child was born of a mother and father, it took a whole tribe or community to raise a child and teach them invaluable lessons.

To think that only one person could be responsible for such an enormous task of raising a child was like putting only a few stars in the sky. This was ludicrous, as how would it be possible to navigate with only a handful of stars? Yet, each person and each star was unique and shone their brilliance and light upon the life of a child. In this way, they all contributed to helping them navigate their journey through life; as well as helping them become well-rounded and 'whole' members of the community.

Zonta sweetly smiled as she watched her beloved father sit by the fire with the boys. With each boy perched on one of grandfather's knees, they would gaze in wide-eyed wonder as they listened quietly to the older members of the tribe. Observing how each person listened carefully and did not interrupt or talk over one another demonstrated to the children that true politeness was defined not in words, but by actions.

Zonta's father loved to take the twins exploring. As they sat upon the ground, their grandfather would pat the soil next to them and say that it was their privilege to be allowed to sit in the lap of beloved

Mother Earth. He stressed to his grandsons, "We are all born from her. Treat your Mother Earth well, because when we all pass, we will return to her."

In this way, the boys grew older with Mother Nature being a canvas of knowledge, constantly presenting new wonders to them. Whether it was the ingenuity and industry learned from watching ants work together, the cunning way a mother fox carefully teaches her cubs to hunt, or how to discern and use the clear signs of the changing of the seasons, these were all invaluable lessons. In their first decade, the boys were shown that by living with respect for all of Great Spirit's creations, life flowed beautifully and naturally. Whether small like a leaf or a tiny insect, or large like a towering pine, a bear or fearsome storms, they all had a significant meaning and a lesson held within. The twins learned that one had only to sit long enough, focus and observe for the clarity of such wisdom to unfold. In this way, they connected with the natural beauty and rhythms of life.

Although the twins were identical in looks and had been taught similar lessons, their natures were vastly different. Just like his easy birth, Ohiyesa was a content and happy child and life seemed to unfold easily around him. In contrast, his brother Akechta was competitive and jealous. Yet there was something even greater that contrasted these twins. Ohiyesa had been born with the gift of prophecy and Akechta had not.

Even as a young child, he would tell the Elders when it was going to rain or when the buffalo would return to the plains and he would warn them of any imminent danger. This gave Ohiyesa a great deal of recognition and praise at an early age. In order to compete with his brother, Akechta decided to gain recognition by becoming the most powerful, ruthless warrior of the tribe. Harnessing his jealous rage, Akechta would kill bear and mountain lions and proudly bring them back to camp. As a young fighter, he was unrivaled. Absolutely fearless, Aketchta gained great acclaim as a warrior, defending the tribe's people.

As the boys advanced in age, their individual gifts did not go unnoticed by Wachinksapa. The Medicine Man knew that both boys exhibited excellent leadership qualities. It was on their thirteenth birthday that the old man decided to pass down the ancient wisdom that had been handed down to him so long ago and to choose his successor.

As far back as he could remember, old Wachinksapa had always been around healers. His father, grandfather and great-grandfather before him all had the gift of prophecy and an ability to heal with their hands. Coming from such a devoted lineage, he felt a tremendous responsibility and obligation towards the work of helping others to heal.

As a young child, he watched as three generations of healers demonstrated the capacity to channel Great Spirit's Divine energy and then transfer this heightened energy into another. In this way, the patients returned to their spiritual center and their emotional and physical ailments disappeared.

As Wachinksapa's wife had been barren, he had never known the joy of having his own children and did not have a son to pass on his knowledge to the next generation. Thus it was at the age of thirteen that Ohiyesha and Akechta began learning the ancient wisdom from the old healer.

To begin their education, it was arranged that the boys would meet daily in the tent of the wise old sage. On the first day of their lessons, they were silently ushered into the old man's tent, directed to sit across from him, and respectfully waited for him to speak.

Wachinksapa sat stone-faced, completely speechless, and just stared at both boys. Five minutes, ten minutes, thirty minutes, forty-five minutes went by without one word being uttered.

At the end of the hour-long session, the old sage said, "Thank you boys. That is enough teaching for today."

Angrily, Akechta rose to his feet and blurted out, "You did not teach us any lesson today."

Turning towards Ohiyesha, the wise Medicine Man asked him what the lesson was. Smiling with intuitive knowing, Ohiyesha replied, "I believe it is the lesson of patience. For the only way we learn patience is to have patience."

Grinning widely, Wachinksapa patted him on the head and said, "You have done well.' Akechta scowled as the recognition fell once again to his elder brother.

On their next meeting, the twins and the wise Shaman sat around the medicine wheel. The importance and understanding of this powerful symbol was a constant reminder of how to honor one's 'Earth Walk.'

Wachinksapa explained to the boys, "This medicine wheel is a reflection of an individual's weaknesses and strengths. It provides pathways to follow for personal growth. Placed before the entrance of each tent, it provides a constant reminder for everyone in the tribe to work on themselves. In this way, there can never be anger or blame. The wheel teaches us that all lessons are equal; as are the gifts and talents of individuals. Thus, each person must be honored for his or her unique contribution and important connection to the tribe.

"With this acknowledgement comes the understanding that everyone respects each other's views. By following the truths represented in the wheel, everyone is able to follow a pathway of truth, peace and harmony. Like life itself, the circle is never ending."

For many months, the boys were taken out in nature and blindfolded to deepen their senses. Without the aid of sight, their ability to hear strengthened. Their sixth sense of intuitive knowing became elevated and they could easily discern which animals were nearby.

As part of their learning, Wachinksapa set off down the river in a canoe with the twins. Silently drifting along the water, the boys were asked to listen to the voices of nature and to take note of the messages from Mother Earth. The Medicine Man explained that just because the waterfall spoke in an easily-heard thundering voice did not make it any more important than the silent falling of a single leaf. All were significant and sacred, as Great Spirit created them all. Their time spent in nature provided wonderful opportunities to learn about the healing properties of herbs, plants, minerals and crystals.

As time went on, the twins spent much less time with their family as their days were spent from dawn till dusk garnering the ancient wisdom of healing from old Wachinksapa. One day the boys followed the wise Shaman into the tent of a very sick man. Allowing both boys time to assess the man's physical ailment, the healer lit some sage and called the boys outside the tent.

Wachinksapa then slowly said, "Many times illness is like a rare crystal or mineral. What is apparent on the surface is only a small indication of much that is hidden beneath the surface. We do not need to know the nature of a person's illness; as these are all mere symptoms. One's symptoms merely show a deeper hidden cause, and reflect the physical manifestation of an unsettled soul."

Taking a sip of water from a wooden bowl, Wachinksapa wiped his brow. The wise man continued, "In this way, all illnesses are a separation of man from the teachings of Great Spirit. To help heal the root cause of the problem, one must work with the universal principles of Great Spirit and lead the patient back to remembering their sacred space. As healers, we do not need to fix the person, as they are not broken. We help them rekindle their relationship with the spirit world and therefore help them rekindle their special relationship with themselves."

As the old man spoke, his voice wavered, and the boys noticed a tear appearing in the corner of his eye. For the words he lovingly delivered to both boys were the same exact words that his beloved father had imparted to him so many moons ago when he was but a young boy himself.

As the years passed, the old sage started to notice that both boys' voices started to drop and get deeper. Their once small bodies began to shoot towards the sky and fill out with lean, strong muscles.

It was during their most intense time of growth that Wachinksapa stressed to the boys, "Just as your bodies are rapidly growing, your minds must grow to understand the importance of approaching life in four steps. Your first step must always be sacrifice. When you want something in your lives, unless you pay for it deeply, through hard work and patience, you will not appreciate it.

"Your second step should be prayer. The Great Spirit hears all prayers, so remember to pray deeply for what you need in order to show Great Spirit your convictions.

"Your third step is transformation. Have no fear and be prepared to undergo many great changes and challenges to be able to be given what you have prayed for.

"And lastly is the stage of giving thanks. When your prayers have been answered, whether the buffalo have returned to feed your family or a loved one has been healed, you have an obligation to give back in gratitude and appreciation for the kindness of Great Spirit."

The changing seasons saw the twins anticipating their sixteenth year. For it was on this birthday that they would start to learn the sacred traditions of their people. The wise old sage explained to the boys that the White Buffalo Calf Woman gave these sacred rites to the Lakota and they were the foundation for the 'right way' of living.

Sitting around the fire, Wachinksapa reverently began to recount to the twins the sacred story that he had told so many times before.

"A long time ago, a chief sent out two young warriors to hunt for game. Unsuccessful, they climbed a high hill to better see over the country. They watched in amazement as the sky before them stared to darken with storm clouds and then the clouds started to descend to the ground.

"Suddenly, out of the storm clouds, they saw a white buffalo calf approaching them. As it came closer, the young warriors saw the calf change into the most beautiful woman that they had ever seen. She was wearing white buckskins and had a bundle tied to her back. As the two young men looked upon her beauty, one said, 'I will have my way with this beauty and take her as my own.'

"As his lustful thoughts propelled him forward, he disrespectfully stretched out his hand to grab her. A thick, black cloud descended and engulfed him. When the cloud arose, there was nothing left but a pile of bones with snakes slithering over them. Seeing his friend's skeleton, the other warrior dropped to his knees and prayed. The White Buffalo Calf Woman then said, 'Go to your people and instruct them to prepare for my arrival. In four days time, I shall bring them a sacred bundle. Tell them they must gather together and form their village in a circle. For the circle is sacred to me.' The warrior then watched as the woman turned back into a white buffalo calf and was suddenly carried up and swept away by a large, black cloud.

"After the tribe's people had made preparations for her arrival, she came to the village as promised, carrying the sacred bundle in her arms. Unwrapping it, she presented the sacred pipe to the tribe. Grasping the stem with her right hand and the bowl with her left, the White Buffalo Calf Woman showed the people of the tribe the use of the pipe. Filling it with red willow bark tobacco, she walked around in a circle four times, which represented the journey of the great circle of life.

"She explained that the smoke that rose from the bowl was the breath of Great Spirit. She taught the people the pipe-filling song and showed them how to lift the pipe to the heavens to Great Spirit and down to Mother Earth and then to the four directions. On completion of these, White Buffalo Calf Woman said, 'This holy pipe will help your people walk a sacred life. With your feet anchored firmly on the ground and the smoke from the pipe rising to Heaven, you will build a bridge between the Sacred above and the Sacred below.' Pointing to the engraving of circles on the bowl of the pipe she said, 'These seven circles will remind you to practice these seven new and sacred ceremonies.'

"She then spoke to the women of the tribe, explaining that their contributions kept the tribe alive and were every bit as great as the contributions of the great male warriors. She stressed how both men and women would create the pipe. The men carved the bowl and the stem, while the women decorated it with colored quills. When they joined as man and wife, they held the pipe at the same time, and a red cloth was wrapped around their hands, binding them together for life.

"She then handed the pipe over to the chief. 'You will be the first keeper of the pipe. You must ensure that each generation knows fully about its importance and choose wisely those who will ensure its safe-keeping.'

"White Buffalo Calf Woman then went to talk to the children and explained the importance of caring for and loving animals, being respectful to all things in nature and living in harmony with their surroundings. 'Remember,' she said, 'the Earth is your grandmother and mother and you must not change anything upon the land. The animals of the earth are your brothers and sisters and should be treated with respect.'

"It was on the morning of the second day that she began teaching about the seven sacred ceremonies. Selecting a group of men, she instructed them on how to construct a sweat lodge and taught songs and chants for performing the Purification ceremony. She then taught them the Healing ceremony and showed them which roots, plants and herbs heal all illnesses. With this knowledge, these men gained much respect and honor from the tribe.

"On the third day, White Buffalo Calf Woman demonstrated three more ceremonies: Marriage, Naming and The Making of Relatives. These ceremonies ensured that the sacred bond between man and wife would be honored and that only truly beautiful names would be chosen to become fully in alignment with Great Spirit. The Making of Relatives ceremony would ensure that the children and those of different tribes would always have a sense of belonging and togetherness.

"The next ceremony involved a gathering together of the men of the tribe, where they were instructed on how to conduct a Vision ceremony by the holy men. Through sweat lodges and rites of purification, they helped the men find their own spirit guides who would help them in their vision quest.

"Lastly, on the morning of the fourth day, White Buffalo Calf Woman showed the people the Sun Dance ceremony. By coming together at the time of the summer solstice, their four-day ritualistic dancing and prayers would be directed towards ending all suffering. Whether the suffering was symbolic or spiritual, from the past or present day, this powerful dance sent out an energetic message to end all fighting and pain upon the Earth.

"Having finished the teaching of the seven sacred ceremonies, White Buffalo Calf Woman left the village. As the tribe's people watched her leave, they saw her change into a white buffalo calf. As the calf bowed to the four corners of the Earth, it then disappeared."

Over time, both boys helped as apprentices as they practiced the sacred rites. By performing the Healing ceremony, they helped the deceased loved ones of the tribe cross over peacefully into the realm of the Great Spirit. By providing comfort and celebrating a departed's life, the boys helped the family deal with death and to find closure.

To help guide people who were in spiritual crisis, the boys performed powerful Purification ceremonies that cleansed a person's spirit and gave the individual renewed insight and clarity. And they lead others in vision quests in order to bring a participant to a new level of awareness of himself and his place in the larger world. In this way, the person was drawn closer to connecting with Great Spirit.

Sitting in the old man's tent one day, the boys saw the Shaman carefully pick up a box and put it on his lap. Opening the box, he gently took out a piece of cloth and started to carefully unwrap it. There, inside, was a red clay pipe. Holding out the pipe to the boys, the old man spoke. "The pipe ceremony that you are about to learn is the sacred ritual for connecting spiritual and physical worlds. There is nothing more sacred as it is the link between Earth and Sky."

As the Shaman filled the bowl of the pipe with tobacco, he explained, "The Great Spirit connects best with those also of spirit. Therefore, the pipe becomes our prayers in physical form and its smoke becomes our words. It travels out, touches everything and mingles easily with all that there is."

He told them that tobacco is used to connect the two worlds because the roots of the tobacco plant are firmly connected to Mother

Earth, yet its smoke rises up into the heavens. This ceremony was important to all treaty-making because it invoked an unbreakable bond with the energies of the Universe, Great Spirit creator and the union between earthly and spiritual realms. That is why it was unimaginable to conceive that a Native American would break his word after smoking the peace pipe.

As the pipe was passed to each boy, they reverently followed the Sage's directions.

"Remember always to call upon and thank the six energies. Call upon the power of the West and thank it for the life-giving rains and the spirit world. Call upon the power of the North, with its source of endurance, honesty, strength and truthfulness. These are qualities that assure a good journey through life.

"Call upon the power of the East. The sun rises in the East and brings forth knowledge, which prevents us from being ignorant and doing harm to ourselves and others. Call to the power of the South, which brings forth growth and bounty. After the four directions have been acknowledged, touch the pipe to the ground as an offering to Mother Earth's life-giving energies."

Suddenly the old Shaman went quiet. After awhile, he reverently spoke again. "And lastly, boys, hold the pipe up to the Great Spirit in the sky to connect with the unexplainable source of all life, and say, 'Oh Great Spirit, I thank you for the six powers of the Universe'."

The pipe was silently passed around until all the tobacco was finished. The ashes were then sprinkled to the ground as an offering to Mother Earth. Smiling broadly at both boys, the old sage knew that the time was drawing near to pick a successor for his position as Medicine Man.

Bringing herself back to the present moment of great celebration, Zonta wiped the tears away from her face, and looked on with motherly pride as the old Shaman lifted up his hand to speak. As Wachinksapa waited for silence, he scanned over his beloved tribe through bleary, tired eyes. He smiled as he recognized all the individuals whom he had helped in his long service as Medicine Man to the tribe.

Clearing his throat, the old man spoke slowly. "I have had the great privilege to watch these two brothers grow and learn the spiritual laws. Both Ohiyesha and Akechta have shown respect and praise for the Great Spirit Creator. They have shown generosity, reverence, true courage and dignity and these are all ways of 'right living' in alignment with the teaching of Great Spirit. Yet, there is one area that separates these almost inseparable twins. For the most important aspect of right living is internal peace and self-control. To be a Medicine Man, one must be able to be in the world, but not of it.

"This constant connection to the spirit world enables a healer to be able to bring the magic and miracles from the Creator down to assist the tribe on Mother Earth. A Medicine Man knows that he has been made in the perfect image of the Creator; he does not have to be in competition with anyone, yet this is the one aspect that has separated these two boys."

Turning to face the twins, the old sage said, "Akechta, as a warrior you are unrivaled. But your soul will always be unsettled because of your competition with your brother. This is the reason why I have chosen Ohiyesha as my apprentice. He will be by my side until I am called to go home to Great Spirit. It will be upon my passing that Ohiyesha will be the next Medicine Man of the tribe."

As the announcement was made, the tribe stepped forward to congratulate Ohiyesha, as Akechta stood in silent defiance. As his parents approached him, Akechta was quick to reply, "I'm so glad that I don't have to waste precious time healing the sick. It would take time away from hunting and really protecting the tribe."

Noticing that Akechta's voice wavered as he spoke, his mother leaned forward to hug her son but he pulled back and quickly walked away.

In the many months that followed, Akechta chose to stay away from the tribe and live in the forest. He couldn't bear to watch as the bond between the old sage and his brother grew stronger. The channeling of his jealous rage into increased hunting and wanton killing only seemed to fuel the hatred that steadily grew towards his brother.

Over time, deep winter blanketed the camp and the frigid days only seemed to mirror the coldness that had settled within Akechta's heart. It was on just such a cold, moonless night that Akechta decided to seek revenge and kill his brother Ohiyesha.

Taking advantage of the night's darkened skies; Akechta was able to sneak undetected towards his brother's tent. As he quietly entered, his keen eyesight made out his brother's sleeping form. Raising his hunting knife above his head, he plunged the blade deep through the blankets. Suddenly, the painful cries of old Wachinksapa could be heard throughout the camp. With his declining health, the Medicine Man had moved into Ohiyesha's tent and was now under his apprentice's constant care.

Akechta looked closely at his victim's face. "Old man!" he cried out in surprise at the realization of his fatal mistake. He watched in horrified silence as the old sage's wrinkled hands tried in vain to pull the weapon from his chest.

Recognizing Aketcha's face, Wachinksapa bit down hard on his lip, more in response to the pain of betrayal than any physical pain. As his life's blood slowly seeped from his aged body, Wachinksapa suddenly heard a familiar, beloved voice. "Remember, Wachinksapa, as healers we do not need to fix this person, as he is not broken. He needs to rekindle his relationship with the spirit world and this will help him rekindle his special relationship with himself."

As Wachinksapa's father appeared before him attired in full ceremonial dress, tears of utter joy streamed down the old man's weathered face. His father held out his hand to him. "Come, my son, it is time to go to Great Spirit." And with those words, the two healers stepped into the tunnel.

11

Heaven – Our True Angelic Nature

As they advanced towards the light, Wachinksapa felt younger and stronger; all the burdens of age and his life's challenges steadily erased. With the weariness of old age melting away from his tired bones, it felt like the warmth of spring thawing winter's ice, revealing new life beneath the surface. He was amazed how his once bleary vision became sharp and clear.

Arriving at the end of the tunnel, Wachinksapa stepped on to the platform. He noticed that he was no longer stooped over. He was surprised that he stood erect and held his head high as he once did as a young warrior. In front of him were the much-loved plains and forests in which he grew up and the largest celebration that his eyes had ever seen. There to greet him was almost a century's worth of cherished friends and family.

The women had prepared a 'coming home' feast and the men had made gifts for his arrival. Wachinksapa's heart filled with joy as he sat in a huge circle surrounded by his tribe. Passing the pipe around, they laughed and shared incidents and stories of their lives together. Suddenly, a form started to appear in the middle of the circle and slowly its shape became more defined.

The form was that of a small, snowy white buffalo calf. The significance of this wondrous miracle did not escape anyone's notice, and all eyes were riveted on its presence. As soon as it appeared, the calf started to change form into a beautiful woman. This was the White Buffalo Calf Woman that had been foretold in the legend.

Walking towards Wachinksapa, she stretched out her hand to him and spoke. "Come, great warrior; allow me the privilege of walking together for awhile."

Nimbly rising to his feet, Wachinksapa noticed that his movements were quick and sharp. Taking White Buffalo Calf Woman's hand, they proceeded to walk towards the forest. As they walked on a path wending its way through the beautiful sights and sounds of nature, Wachinksapa plucked up enough courage to speak to this sacred lady. "I am so honored, dear lady, that you have asked me to walk with you."

She replied, "The honor is mine, Wachinksapa. It is you who has lived a life that was a direct reflection of all my teachings, and for that I thank you." As she spoke those words, they came upon a clearing in the forest and there in front of them was the Hall of Justice. "I must leave you here, for you must proceed on your own."

Wachinksapa climbed the marble steps and as he arrived at the top, he turned around just in time to see White Buffalo Calf Woman slowly fade away.

Once inside the great Hall, Wachinksapa watched the review of his life. For nearly a century, this wise Medicine Man had helped so many people in the tribe. He watched as scene after scene showed him presiding over births, marriages, purification rites and vision quests. He was there to assist Great Spirit in healing and restoring people's health. And he was also there to hold their hands and sit with Great Spirit as individuals were called to cross over in peace. His eyes misted over as he watched and relived the crossing over of his beloved wife of fifty years. His tears flowed freely as he watched how he tenderly cradled his beautiful wife in his arms and chanted prayers to ensure a safe journey home to Great Spirit.

When his review was over, he sat in silence for a very long time, remembering the flood of memories from his long life. Looking up, he noticed that the doors had started to open as a signal for him to proceed to the Hall of Akashic Records.

In response to his thoughts, the great Hall towered in front of him. Before entering the huge marble building, he stopped, turned towards the Great Sun, and looked up and then down. In reverent, whispered words, as if he was uttering them for the last time, he said, "Beautiful Mother Earth and Beloved Father Sky, thank you for blessing me with such an extraordinary, wonderful life."

Slowly he bowed to the powers of the West, the North, the South and the East. Upon completion of expressing his gratitude, he walked down the corridor towards the grand Hall. As the semi-circle of the wise Etheric Council came into view, he instinctively stopped and respectfully waited for them to speak first.

The Council looked over their rimmed glasses and spoke. "Welcome Home, Ariel. It is so good to have you back with us once more." Unlike other times, Ariel did not have to be awakened to know who she really was. Watching her calm demeanor and examining her carefully, the Council continued, "You are somehow different, my dear, more serene and at peace than the other times that you have returned Home. Tell us what you are experiencing."

Ariel replied as a knowing smile broke across her face, "Thank you. It is good to be back and held in the loving energies of so many dear ones. Yet, in many ways, I feel as if I never left, for I experienced the same things on Earth as I did in Heaven. When I left here, I went back conscious and awakened in full knowledge of what it means to live a spiritual life. In so doing, I lived each moment with my face turned towards God, knowing that my highest gift was to be of service through him."

As she spoke, the Etheric Council noticed a glow of light that was outlining Ariel. She continued, "Every other time that I have returned Home, it felt so good to unburden myself and shed my Earthly incarnation. Yet, I now know that I am and always will be Wachinksapa, and he is always me." Pausing for a moment, Ariel then continued, "For you see beloved Elders, I Am Ankhesenamun, I Am

Annabel Rose MacDonald, I Am Angelica, I Am Adetoun, and I Am Wachinksapa and they are all me. I Am all cultures, I Am all tribes, and I Am all races, genders and nations. I Am one with God and one with all."

The Etheric Council looked on in amazement as a huge halo of white light emanated from around her. Ariel began to powerfully connect with the Divine within. The Council knew that they were witnessing Ariel realizing her true, Divine angelic nature.

With tears flowing down her cheeks, she proudly replied in a voice that was so much larger than her small frame. "I Am that I Am. And from this day forward, I will commit myself to being in the service of God because there is nothing more a soul can ever hope to strive for."

With beaming smiles, the Etheric Council picked up a long quill pen, and signed and sealed the contract of her last incarnation. Closing up her Book of Life, they said, "It is by no accident that you are called Ariel, for the meaning of your name is 'Lion of God.' With your devotion, courage and strength, from this day forward, Ariel, you will serve as one of God's angels and help reawaken others to living their spiritual awareness. By helping and giving permission to others to shine brightly, the world's love, harmony and peace will increase, one person at a time."

Bowing to the Elders, Angel Ariel turned and walked down the corridor of the great columned building. With each step she took, she felt as though everything that she had ever done and every incarnation that she had ever lived, had been leading up to this moment. With this thought, her steps started to quicken. She felt so alive, as if born for the first time. She longed to start helping others to reawaken to the same glorious realization of unity and connectedness. The hurried pace of her steps mirrored her unbridled excitement, as she couldn't wait to get started.

Bursting through the doors of the great Hall, she ran down the steps. Jumping from the last step, she realized that she didn't know where she was going, or how she was going to implement her newfound knowledge. As she stood, unsure, in the courtyard, she felt a slight breeze and became aware of a beautiful scent of roses. Standing very still, she felt a presence drawing near to her. Out of nowhere, she then heard the words, "When the student is ready, the Master appears."

In an instant, a form started to take shape; as if carefully painted by an exacting artist. A tall and slender barefoot Chinese woman started to emerge out of the air. Her features were delicate as if chiseled in fine porcelain and her lithe figure was draped in an embroidered white flowing robe.

A white hood gently adorned the top of her head. In one hand, she carried an upturned vase and the other held a book. On her shoulder sat a white dove. As she approached Angel Ariel, her movements were graceful and elegant.

"Greetings, Angel Ariel. My name is Quan Yin. I am but one of the Ascended Masters." As she spoke, her tones had a soothing, melodic quality; its rhythmic cadence sounding like sweet music. "I have come as your guide, to help you be of service to others."

Captivated by Quan Yin's gentle, flowing movements, Angel Ariel's heart connected with her tender energies. Finding her voice, Angel Ariel said, "Excuse me, but what is an Ascended Master?"

Stepping forward, Quan Yin gently bowed. "Let us take a walk through the lovely gardens, while I explain." Passing by the flowers that were bursting with vibrant colors, Quan Yin carefully selected each word, as if it were a rare gem. "Ascended Masters are enlightened spiritual beings who once lived on the Earth plane. Over numerous incarnations, we have shown steadfast devotion and perseverance to fulfilling our mission and reason for being."

With a stunned look, Angel Ariel quickly said, "But how can there be one mission, one reason for being? In each one of my lifetimes, I was a different person and I wrote out a different contract for that particular life."

Quan Yin gently smiled. "You are absolutely correct. Yet, underlying each one of those lives was the same exact mission. It was your Divine plan to be self-realized and to ascend back to Divine

Source, reuniting you with Spirit. Peace within and self-realization is the absolute awareness of our inseparable union with God.

"Once we become awakened to this, then we can clearly separate from our egos and there ceases to be constant struggles in our lives. A deep knowing settles in our consciousness that we have always been Divine and we feel an overwhelming sense of security, peace and abundance. Once this happens, Angel Ariel, all darkness and negative karma from the physical body is transformed into pure light; just take a look at your hands."

Looking down, Angel Ariel saw a soft glow and felt a strong, pulsating energy emanating from her fingertips. Angel Ariel remarked, "So you were once human?"

"Yes, that is right. The Ascended Masters come from every era, religion and culture, yet we are united as 'The Great White Brotherhood'."

"White?"

"The term 'white' does not mean race, but refers to the immense white light that surrounds our forms."

Angel Ariel was silent as she was digesting all that Quan Yin had told her. A question then occurred to her. "So you don't have to go back to Earth and can remain in Heaven?"

"Well, the Elders do tell us that, as souls, we never 'have to' go back to the Earth plane. But it is necessary if one still wishes to be self-realized and learn their lessons. As Ascended Masters, we have transcended the need for the birth/death cycle."

Walking over to one of the carved benches in the garden, Quan Yin's form seemed to float down onto the bench. Angel Ariel watched her silently breathe in the restful, nurturing energies of nature. Slowly, a wistful, far-away gaze settled on her face.

"In my own lifetimes, I experienced great sacrifice and great love, which eventually earned me the right to enter Paradise. Yet, just as I was about to enter the gates of Heaven, I heard a cry of anguish from the Earth below. I knew that I could never rest comfortably in eternal bliss, knowing that people were still suffering. It was then that

I decided to devote myself to the salvation of others from their misery.

"I hear the cries from the human world and I hear their prayers, and comfort those in pain. I compassionately give my life over to help with the afflictions of humanity."

Feeling an overwhelming need to shed tears, Angel Ariel wiped the corners of her eyes and said, "That is so noble of you."

"I am nothing special, for there are many Ascended Masters who chose to remain connected with souls on Earth. They guide them to self-transcendence, which the Masters have already achieved." Rising from the bench, Quan Yin continued along the path. "Angel Ariel, you have now reached an important threshold in your spiritual awakening. For it is only by being fully awakened ourselves, can we then go on to help others awaken."

Stopping and gently drawing in a long breath, Quan Yin continued, "On a final note for today, I can tell you that you don't have to be an Ascended Master to have access to spiritual knowledge. All one needs to do is to ask to be told and shown what you need to further your spiritual development. In this way, one may receive light, healing, blessing and instructions on fulfilling one's unique and Divine mission. These soft whisperings from Spirit are available to all, but few take the time to still themselves long enough to listen for them."

As if on cue, the path abruptly ended. Looking down, Quan Yin said, "Just as the path has finished, so has our time together come to an end. My advice for you is to go my child—rest, play and have fun. You will be contacted when it is time to advance on the next steps of your journey and to meet with three very important guides."

As Quan Yin slowly started to fade from view, Angel Ariel quickly said, "I forgot to ask—why do you carry a book, a vase and a dove?"

Quan Yin's reply floated to Ariel as if from far away. "The vase holds the precious nectar of compassion, the dove is for eternal peace and the book contains the highest teachings, those of God." And with that, Quan Yin faded from view and Angel Ariel was once again alone in the garden.

Sitting down on one of the carved benches surrounded by the flowers, Angel Ariel was so excited about her meeting with Quan Yin. To make sure it was not merely a dream, she looked down at her hands. Sure enough, they still were emitting a beautiful golden glow. With her newly-realized spiritual wisdom and true angelic nature, she desperately wanted to get started by being an angel to help others.

She thought, "Quan Yin said all I need to do now is just rest, play and have fun."

It was then that her thoughts turned to her beloved Kiel. Tuning in to her Twin Flame, she knew that he was experiencing another incarnation on Earth and it would be some time before they would see each other again. She decided that she could not bear to go to their beautiful Victorian home without him.

As soon as she decided against it, the thought of her Italian villa came into mind. Without realizing it, Angel Ariel said out loud, "I love my villa, but for some reason it just doesn't seem the place to be right now. Oh! I'm so confused."

Immediately she heard a tiny voice that spoke with a Cockney accent. "When I'm confused it's because I am finkin' wiv me 'ead and not me 'eart."

Quickly looking around, Angel Ariel searched for the owner of the voice, but saw that she was very much alone. Sitting very still, her ears detected a faint buzzing noise. Following the sound, she knelt down in front of the flowers until her face was almost touching the blooms.

Staring at the petals, Angel Ariel saw a tiny faerie hovering in midair. The faerie's wings were beating so quickly they could not be seen, which reminded her of the wings of hummingbirds. And with her thought, several hummingbirds appeared and were pushing and shoving to get the nectar from one of the big blossoms. As they were jostling for position, one of them bumped the faerie.

"Hey, guys! Play nice! Remember this is 'eaven and there is plenty of nectar for everyone."

Turning her attention to Angel Ariel's startled face, the faerie's wings stopped beating and she gently drifted down onto one of the flowers. The tiny weight of her body hardly made an impression on the petal.

"Now, what was we discussin'?" proclaimed the wee little person. "Aw, that's right. It's times like these that one must fink with one's 'eart. Tell me, girlie, what do you really want to do, not what you fink you oughta be doin?"

Angel Ariel giggled out loud at the sight and sound of this tiny being, just too precious to behold. The faerie had masses of blonde, tight-knit curls that seemed to be fighting for position on her head. As the faerie spoke, the vibrations from her voice made her curls dance up and down. She was wearing a flowing gown of the palest lavender and her wings looked as if they had been laced with silver threads.

Walking closely to the edge of the petal, the faerie smoothed out her gown that had been crinkled by the hummingbirds. "While yer finkin' of an answer to me question let me introduce meself." She stretched forth her tiny hand. "Me name's Violet and to be sure, there ain't nofin' that is shrinkin' about me." As she said this, she proudly rose to her full height of two inches and threw back her shoulders.

Not to seem rude, Angel Ariel contained her urge to burst out laughing. "It is an honor and a pleasure to make your acquaintance, Violet. I'm Angel Ariel."

The wee faerie continued, "Now that you found yer voice, wot is it that ye really want to be doin'?"

Angel Ariel started to think about her long life of service in her last incarnation. As Wachinksapa the Medicine Man, every day had been spent in constant devotion to helping and healing others. Though it had been a wonderful life, there was very little time for diversion of any sort. Leaning forward again, Angel Ariel let out a huge sigh and her breath knocked the faerie over.

Getting to her feet and straightening out her dress again, Violet cried, "Steady on, girl, I asked for an answer, not a 'urricane."

"Sorry about that. You know, Violet, if I really have to be honest, Quan Yin was right. All I want to do now is to rest, play and have fun."

At those words, Violet's wings began to beat quickly and lifted her off the petal. Excitedly, she started to dart around Angel Ariel's head. "Yippee, and that's zactly wot Quan Yin had in mind when she sent me to you." She whizzed back and forth, slowed down her wing speed and then landed on a rose. "Okay, now close your eyes and fink about havin' fun and playin' in a nice, restful place."

As Angel Ariel closed her eyes, she felt what it would be like to be totally relaxed and playful. As she let these feelings settle into her heart, a beautiful image immediately started to paint itself in front of her.

12

Heaven – Discovering
Our Divine Passion

Appearing before her eyes was a long wall covered with bright pink geraniums. Tiny hummingbirds were darting in and out of the flowers. Staring at the vision that was manifesting from her thoughts, Angel Ariel watched as the middle of the wall was suddenly erased and three red steps were painted in. The top step continued along a red cement pathway that divided a small lawn of emerald green grass.

A paintbrush appeared out of nowhere and began to drip brown and green colors into the air. With steady care and attention, the paintbrush painted several fruit trees bearing plums, lemons, oranges, pears and limes. This told Angel Ariel that her new home would provide a great deal of sweetness and abundance.

The paintbrush then continued the red path up another three long steps, which lead to a bright red porch and an adorable blue and white cottage. Gleaming white wicker furniture appeared with overstuffed red-and-white striped cushions. Angel Ariel sighed, thinking how lovely a place it would be to sit on a cool evening and look out at beautiful scenery. In response to her thoughts, a bright red cashmere blanket draped itself over one of the wicker chairs and a vista suddenly appeared overlooking hills in the distance.

Thinking of her favorite flowers, the paintbrush snapped to

attention, painting beautiful rose bushes along the side of the house.

Finishing off the last of the delicate petals, the paintbrush heaved a sigh and came to rest in the green grass.

Standing in front of her storybook cottage, Angel Ariel felt like something was missing. She heard Violet's tiny voice whispering in her ear. "Come on, girlie, concentrate 'arder on 'avin' fun."

Shutting her eyes and furrowing her brow, Angel Ariel focused on playing. Once more, the paintbrush started to come alive. Dripping cotton candy pink paint, the brush danced around so quickly that Angel Ariel had a great deal of trouble following it. When it finally came to a stop, there in the front yard appeared a pink bicycle with pink streamers, a pink basket and a bell.

As she turned and faced away from her cottage, she looked out on a seaside town filled with flowers. Nestled at the foothills of a mountain range and bordered by the ocean, her fairytale-like town had the most relaxing and welcoming of energies.

With great excitement, Angel Ariel grasped the doorknob and entered her new home. She stepped into a large lounge room with comfy purple sofas in front of a cozy fireplace. To her right was an elegant baby grand piano. The shiny white keys looked like smiling teeth, encouraging and welcoming her to compose.

As she looked left, there appeared a sun-filled dining room and kitchen. Walking to the other side of the house, she found several more rooms, including an office at the front of the cottage. But, this office was anything but formal. Although it had a desk and two chairs, it was filled with angel statues and crystals of every description winking and twinkling their energies at her.

As Angel Ariel walked back into the lounge, a door appeared at the end of the room. Stepping through the door, she saw her bedroom complete with a beautiful bed dressed in a plush comforter of pale pink lace with pink pillows resting against the headboard. In the corner was an elegant vanity table and the whole room was filled with the perfumed scent of roses and vanilla.

Watching all of this unfold before her eyes, Violet was unable to contain herself, and excitedly flew into the bedroom. Trying to quickly land on the dressing table, she skidded along the surface and landed head first in the talcum powder. As a fine mist of white powder settled all around, she got up and shook off her wings.

Trying to divert attention away from the rather wayward landing, Violet exclaimed, "Caw blimey me dear, look what you can do when you put your mind and your 'eart to what you truly want."

But there was no reply.

As Violet turned around, she saw Angel Ariel snuggled in the middle of the soft pink pillows, as she had fallen fast asleep.

The next day saw yet another picture-perfect sunny day in the seaside town of Santa Barbara, California. Violet had woken early and was pacing back and forth outside the bedroom. She knew that Angel Ariel was tired, but she had underestimated her new friend's exhaustion. Leaning up against Angel Ariel's bedroom door, the little faerie's patience was wearing quite thin as she crossed her arms and frowned.

Just then, the door opened and Violet fell into the bedroom. Picking herself up, she grumbled, "Well, it's about time."

Angel Ariel rubbed her eyes. "I'm so sorry, Violet. I had no idea that I was so weary."

Violet stamped her foot impatiently, saying, "It's not so much for meself, but ye know there has been someone else who is just bustin' to see you." Violet flew up to Angel Ariel's face and took a strand of her hair. Tugging on it, both of them went in the direction of the porch.

As Angel Ariel opened the front door, her arms were suddenly full of brown fur. Her beautiful little Yorkshire terrier, Cleo, had been waiting patiently for her to awaken. Angel Ariel hugged her little friend tightly. "How could I have possibly forgotten to draw you in my picture?"

Violet held her sides and giggled. "You must 'ave bin, scuse the expression, dog tired!"

From that day on, the three friends were inseparable, exploring the beautiful foreshore and the many charms of her fairytale village.

As Angel Ariel rode her bicycle, Cleo sat in the basket, trying to catch the breeze with her tongue. Always eager for a race, Violet would fly alongside the bicycle and try to keep pace. After they had their fill of exploring the beaches, Angel Ariel put on her hiking boots and ventured along the mountain tracks. Stopping by a clear, flowing stream, Cleo would bend over to try to get a drink and would end up toppling over into the water. But, she always made sure to share with others by vigorously shaking herself next to Violet and Angel Ariel.

One night as Cleo and Angel Ariel sat on the purple sofa, they listened as Violet tried to play a tune on the piano, jumping from key to key. Completely exhausted after several notes, the little faerie collapsed in a heap.

"Here, let me help you," said Angel Ariel. She began to play. While the two girls were making beautiful music together, Cleo was the first to notice a strange golden light that was coming from the hallway, and the little pup began to growl. Following the bright light, Angel Ariel saw that it was coming from underneath her office door.

Slowly easing the door open, she discovered that the radiant light was coming from a pen on the desk. "Funny," she thought, "I could have sworn that the desk had been completely clear." While she stared at the strange light, Angel Ariel felt compelled to sit down and pick up the pen. As if this were the cue that the pen had been waiting for, a notebook appeared and Angel Ariel and the pen began to write.

Her hand seemed to take on a life of its own as words effortlessly appeared on the page. Trying to keep pace while the words streamed forth from the pen, Angel Ariel was astonished as she became aware of what she was writing.

The pregnant full moon guided the Egyptian barge over the mirror-like surface of the River Nile. .... Suddenly, Angel Ariel realized that she was writing about her past incarnation; her life and early death as Ankhesenamun flowed freely onto the pages.

Although these memories may have been previously filled with pain, she was able to distance herself from her feelings and write about her lives from a higher perspective. As soon as she had recorded her life as the Egyptian Princess, the pen continued on to her next life as Annabel Rose MacDonald. The pen didn't halt as it described the harsh conditions of her life as a healer and the cruel and horrific death she suffered being burned at the stake.

Both Violet and Cleo sat in the doorway of the office and watched as Angel Ariel wrote feverishly. As the pen finished with the story of Annabel Rose MacDonald, it stopped as if to take a breath.

Perched on top of Cleo's head, Violet leaned into the room, expecting their friend to come and play. Yet that short breath was all that the pen needed to become re-energized, as it quickly went on to Angelica's life of privilege as a Courtesan. Feeling less burdened after describing her heavy, suppressed life as a serf, the labored strokes of the pen took on a lighter movement.

It swayed and skipped, as if dancing to a gavotte, as it told the story of Angelica's life in Venice, Italy. The pen was inspired by Angel Ariel's happy feelings, remembering what it felt like to be adored and respected for her intelligence. Now it was Angel Ariel's turn to stop and take a deep breath.

She halted for a moment as she reflected on the fact that, in those times, a woman could only gain access to knowledge if she prostituted herself as a whore. The pen spent an inordinate amount of time describing the lavish jewels, elegant gowns and sumptuous meals. Angel Ariel wondered why the pen slowed down and carefully detailed her wealth and her relaxed life of joy and ease. As Angelica breathed her last breath of life on Earth and sank back into her exquisitely-embroidered silk bed linens, Angel Ariel felt the pen pause and then stop. She tried to write, but the pen held back; hesitating to write the next chapter.

Angel Ariel thought, "The pen must have spent such a long time retelling the joyous life of Angelica, because it knew that it would be difficult to record the next life of cruelty and despair that she experienced as a slave." The pen bowed forward, as if nodding in agreement.

Slowly, the pen started to write the heartbreaking life of Adetoun and her journey into hell as a slave. It retold in detail of being ripped from her loving family and taken from her beloved homeland as she and her Aunt Ngozi were transported like cargo. The pen seemed to drip tears of ink and constantly stopped and shook itself, as if it were deeply sobbing and catching its breath in order to continue the harrowing tale.

Squeezing out the last words as Eliza's body lay battered and lifeless at the hand of her owner, Massa Randolph, Angel Ariel sat exhausted; seemingly lifeless herself.

Taking a few deep breaths as if to clear her lungs of the fetid air of slavery, Angel Ariel turned her thoughts to her next incarnation as the wise Medicine Man, Wachinksapa.

In an instant, she felt her spirits begin to rise and hope re-entered her soul. The pen started to glow once more and tugged on her arm to start writing again. With renewed positive feelings, it danced across the page faster than ever, sensing that the quicker it wrote about the wonderful life of service of Wachinksapa, the sooner it could distance itself from the sadness of the former life as a slave.

As the pen described and painted the Medicine Man's love and deep connection to Mother Earth, Angel Ariel sensed once again the connection of White Buffalo Calf Woman's wisdom and alignment to Great Spirit. The noticeable slowing down of the pen interrupted her reverie and she watched as the golden glow around it began to change color.

The golden hue that had been radiating from the pen was replaced by a brilliant white glow, and its radiance filled the room. With the white rays illuminating every corner of the office, Angel Ariel was able to easily discern the outlines of many applauding angels. Their presence and loving thoughts conveyed the importance of recording her knowledge and the truth about our one true Home and the continuation of life behind the veil.

Encouraged by the angels, she wrote about the wonderful journey that souls get to take upon choosing to incarnate to Earth. She first wrote about the meeting we all get to have with the wise Etheric Council and the writing of our contracts. Angel Ariel detailed how all souls not only choose the outline of their lives, they choose other souls and their characteristics which help them best learn their lessons. She penned in detail that once we incarnate, we are never alone, as angels and spirit guides protect, guide and love us on our new journey.

Thinking back to each one of her incarnations, Angel Ariel smiled. At the end of each of her lives, when her soul had lifted from its physical form, an angelic guide was always present to help her Spirit on its journey back Home.

The pen then began to skip and hop, as if keeping time in a dance. Angel Ariel and the pen felt a lightness and joy, as souls were once again reunited with dear loved ones at their homecoming reunion party. The pen was quick to note that these people at your homecoming party neither condemned nor condoned the life choices that you made while on the Earth. They were merely honoring you for the courage and strength it took to live a physical incarnation in order to further your spiritual growth.

Once we cross over, the pen described in detail the Hall of Justice, where we sit and review the life we just lived in human form. In its description, the pen stressed that there is no judgment whatsoever at one's life review. It is only to see how one chose to live one's incarnation through one's choices.

Continuing, Angel Ariel wrote about how we all come full circle to visit the Etheric Council once again at the Hall of Akashic Records in order to assess the contract of our last incarnation. The pen and Angel Ariel described the ability in Heaven to manifest whatever house one desired and the opportunities to live one's passion and talents through our chosen work.

She beamed as she wrote about the details of her Italian villa, her Victorian home near the ocean, and her adorable cottage in the fairytale village of Santa Barbara.

As there is no time in Heaven, it is difficult to say how long Angel Ariel and the pen co-wrote the story of *One True Home—Behind the*

Veil of Forgetfulness. Yet, as they finished writing the last lines of spiritual knowledge, she heard an angel's choir praising her work. The angels' voices told her that part of her angelic mission would be to help others understand about the wonderful journey that we all get to take. As if on cue, the pen stood up on end, tipped slightly forward, and bowed.

Staring at the book, Angel Ariel wondered what to do with it. She heard soft words whispering in her ear. "You will know when it is the Divine timing to bring forth this knowledge to others."

Walking out of the office, Angel Ariel's sudden appearance startled Violet. "Phew, I was startin' to fink that we was never goin' to play again." The faerie sighed deeply. As Cleo gleefully danced between Angel Ariel's legs, Violet continued, "Wot was you writin'? It must 'ave been important."

"I wrote about my past incarnations, the people I met and the wonderful lessons I've learned. The angels had me include the details of the wonderful journey we all get to take behind the Veil of Forgetfulness." Angel Ariel stopped and laughed aloud. "You know, Violet, you hit the nail on the head because that is exactly how I feel; as if I just completed something of great importance."

Lying in bed that night, Angel Ariel felt light and clear, as if a great responsibility she was carrying had been lifted from her small shoulders.

As the first rays of sunlight danced into her bedroom, she opened up one eye and sensed immediately why she had been drawn to this little cottage. It was here in these peaceful energies surrounded by glorious flowers and hummingbirds that she would write. A slight breeze came in through her bedroom window whispering confirmation of her thoughts.

Each day, Angel Ariel would sit in her sunny pink-and-white office, close her eyes and thank God for her infinite blessings. Feeling complete protection, guidance and love, she took a few long, deep breaths, then waited and listened for the still, small voice of God's creative inspiration to touch her soul.

Within no time, books started to rapidly form with very little effort. Many times, ideas flowed with such ease and fluidity that it was difficult to keep pace with the pen. In fact, while writing she felt like she was a mere guest taken on a wondrous journey. Often, Angel Ariel had no idea what was going to eventuate from her efforts. Being so engrossed in her writing, she allowed God's inspiration to channel through her.

To help regain balance in her life, Angel Ariel had two wonderful helpers to remind her to go outside in the sunshine and play. After many hours of writing, Violet would fly in and buzz around Angel Ariel's head as a reminder to take a break. Cleo would sit patiently with her head on crossed paws and wait for her to stop writing. As soon as Angel Ariel would rise from her chair, Cleo would leap in the air and head for the door.

Life in her little cottage was picture-perfect. Her soul was nourished through her passion for writing. Being with Violet and Cleo allowed the little girl inside her to dance and be spontaneous. Her enormous joy of life also spilled over into her piano-playing. As the melodies drifted out of the little cottage, neighbors passing by would comment on how much they loved her playing. Even the birds gathered on the tree branches chirped along with the music.

It was on one of these picture-perfect mornings that Angel Ariel sat at her desk and thought about the books that she had already completed. Looking down at the book she was working on, she thought, "Not much longer and this one will be completed as well."

Yet this morning, unlike other times, the pen did not seem to share her enthusiasm, as it felt heavy and seemed to be stuck to the desk. Angel Ariel laughed out loud. "Very funny, Violet. Good joke, gluing my pen to the desk." But Violet was nowhere to be seen. Angel Ariel suddenly heard a bird frantically chirping at the top of its lungs. While she tried to focus on her writing, the chirping increased and now seemed to have a sense of urgency about it.

Looking out the window, Angel Ariel saw a tiny bird sitting in a nest on the clothesline. Deciding to go outside and investigate, she drew quite close to the nest. The bird did not move and instead looked straight into her eyes and became even more animated. Violet flew by and landed on a nearby branch. "Caw blimey, you do 'ave a lot to say for yourself. What's all the commotion?"

Angel Ariel replied, "It's trying to tell me something and by the sounds of it, it sure seems important." Tuning in to the frantic chirps, she walked back to her desk and put aside the book that she was working on. Taking some fresh sheets of paper, she felt compelled to write a new story. Lightness returned to the pen, which now floated across the page and danced as if in tune to the meaning behind the frantic chirps.

That was it! Angel Ariel was astounded as she realized that she was writing the tale that the little bird had told her. She watched in amazement as a beautiful story emerged about a lovely lady who kept her faith in God and was rewarded by the blessing of giving birth to a very special daughter named Faith who saw and believed in angels. Page after page emerged as the words tumbled forth and flowed onto the paper. As the story came to an end, the pen came to a halt.

It was then that Angel Ariel could hear swooshing noises coming from the garden. Opening the window to get a better look, a gust of wind blew past her, scattering the pages to the floor. Riding on the gust of wind was Violet, followed closely by five of her faerie friends. Flitting excitedly around the room, Violet landed on the desk. "I just got finished talking to the little bird and he said you could use our help."

Bending over to pick up the pages from the floor, Angel Ariel said, "Are you going to help me put these pages back in order?"

Violet giggled. "Don't be silly. We are here to help illustrate this beautiful story." Reaching into her tiny backpack, she took out some paints and brushes. Scattering them on the desk, Violet giggled again. "OK, girlies, let's 'ave some fun!" They grabbed sheets of paper, dipped their wings in the paint, and began to dive bomb onto the pages, illustrating the bird's wonderful story.

Being so closely connected with nature, the faeries knew exactly what the little bird was saying. As paints flew in all directions and the humming from their busy wings increased, Angel Ariel watched in amazement as beautiful drawings started to form. Darting back and forth, the faeries added detail, whimsy and tender touches to the drawings; bringing life to the words of Angel Ariel's heavenly story.

Within no time, the illustrations had been completed. Yet, in their creative frenzy and excitement, the faeries' artistic freedom had splashed the paints all over the room. Everyone was covered from toe to wing tips in the colors of the rainbow.

Crawling out from under the desk, poor Cleo had not escaped the flying paints. One of her ears was red, one was blue, and a large dollop of yellow paint covered her nose. Angel Ariel laughed out loud, "All right, everyone outside for a wash."

Grabbing the hose, she began to sprinkle the tiny little beings and scrubbed Cleo's fur until all the paint was gone. Lying on the soft grass, the sun's gentle rays warmed and dried them off. Angel Ariel felt such joy and utter contentment. Having completed the bird's story, which she titled *Angels of Faith,* along with all her other books, she felt like she had finished a chapter of her life. She sensed immediately that a new chapter was about to unfold.

That night, the Etheric Council came to her in a dream and asked her if she would like to go on an exciting journey. It would not only be a journey of discovery, but one of remembrance for her as well. Above all, they stressed that they would reveal to her the next step in being of best service to God.

Having completed the important task of bringing forth the knowledge contained in her books, the Elders told her that she was now ready to meet her second guide who would help her along her journey.

It was at that moment that Angel Ariel realized that her friend Violet had been her first guide all along. And it dawned on her the importance of Violet's message on playing and having fun.

Anticipating her new adventure, Angel Ariel awoke in a very excited state the next morning. Wildly throwing the covers off, she leapt out of bed and tipped poor Cleo over the side. The flying covers knocked her beret from the bedpost and it sailed through the air. When the hat came to a rest on its side, a rather dizzy, sleepy-eyed Violet crawled out.

"Blimey, are you tryin' to smother me? Wot is goin' on?"

Angel Ariel replied, "Oh, Violet, the Elders have planned a wonderful journey of discovery and remembrance for me." Watching Violet's happy expression suddenly change, she hesitated before saying, "But it begins today." With the uttering of those words, she became aware that the cottage and everything inside it slowly began to fade from sight.

Violet had known for quite some time that this day would come. Yet she experienced such joy with her kindred friend that she had chosen to ignore it. With this realization, Violet's usual bossy, talkative nature was replaced with a noticeable silence. Two huge puddles of tears formed in her sad eyes and she lowered her head, trying to hide her feelings. Taking her wing and wiping her eyes, she breathed a huge sigh.

"Missy, we sure are goin' to miss you 'eaps." Violet then perked up, shook herself off and said, "But you know in 'eaven's time, you would only be gone two or three weeks at the most. So you'll be back before we can miss you properly. Ain't that right, Cleo?" The puppy stood on her hind legs, danced around and barked in agreement.

Reaching down and giving Cleo a hug, Angel Ariel said, "Thank you, Violet, for all your help, your guidance and love. You will always be with me in my heart. I promise I will never forget to have fun."

Flying up to Angel Ariel's face, Violet gave her a kiss on the cheek. Finding her composure once again, Violet said, "Well, dearie, I hate goodbyes, so I'll just say see ya soon."

Standing on the platform of the transition level, it dawned on Angel Ariel that this was the first time that she would return to Earth without writing a contract. The Etheric Council had told her that, with her enlightened spiritual awareness, she would clearly recognize the signs that she needed to continue her spiritual path. As her name was called, an excited tingle ran through her body. Right before she stepped into the tunnel, she saw Violet's wings waving goodbye.

13

Kimberley, Western Australia, 1963

Emerging from the tunnel, Angel Ariel felt a definite change in the surrounding air. The crisp, fresh breeze of her fairytale village was replaced by an eerie stillness; and the air felt hot and dry. As she concentrated on this change in temperature, a dramatically different landscape began to manifest before her eyes.

A vast ocean appeared and spread out as far as she could see. Ancient rock cliffs began to burst through the surface from the ocean depths, dispersing the water and linking together to form a huge plateau. Sprouting up as if by magic were enormous stretches of open forests and woodlands covering the area with a blanket of green against dark, weathered rock. Fighting to compete with the newly formed landmass, the displaced water from the ocean carved deep tracks, gullies and valleys into the rock. The descent from one rock to the next was so great in some places that it formed a series of steps with beautiful waterfalls cascading into crystal-clear pools.

Before she knew it, Angel Ariel stood in stunned silence by the breathtaking beauty of a remote region of Australia. She was now overlooking the Mitchell Plateau in the northern region of Western Australia known as the Kimberley.

With her attention focused on the stillness in the air, her sixth sense picked up a presence drawing closer. Looking around in all directions, her eyes could not visibly pick up the sight of anyone. Yet her heart told her that someone was out there. Taking her focus off her limited sense of vision, she centered her concentration on her unlimited consciousness. By being receptive to seeing what her eyes could not, someone started to materialize.

Looking on with great curiosity, Angel Ariel watched as a long, narrow opening cut through the air before her. Peeling back this windowed envelope of space and time, a long brown leg appeared through the slit. This was followed by another brown leg attached to a tall, lean torso with long, lithe brown arms. Last to pop through this slender porthole was a mop of wavy black hair and an engaging white grin.

"G'day! I heard you calling me across the great divide. You must have very strong powers." Stretching to his full height of almost six feet, the Aborigine took a step toward Angel Ariel. Holding out his hand, he said, "Struth, scuze me manners. Me names George Jerramala Wunambal."

Smiling and taking his hand, she replied, "My name is Angel Ariel and I don't mean to stare, but I didn't expect that kind of an entrance."

Staring off into thin air, George replied, "Sorry to surprise you, but I was elsewhere when you called." Looking at Angel Ariel's puzzled expression, George asked, "You did ask for a guide, didn't you?"

It was then that Angel Ariel remembered the Council's words: "You will meet three new guides to help you along your journey." Knowing that the Elders arranged for her to be well looked-after on her journey of discovery and remembrance, she replied, "Yes, of course, you're my new guide; nice to meet you."

George looked down at his weathered, wrinkled skin. "I'm not sure how new I am, but I sure am one of the best trackers and guides you'll ever meet. I'll show you some of the oldest, most sacred places on the planet."

As they walked along the plateau, Angel Ariel listened intently as

George's descriptive words painted a vivid picture of the Ngauwudu region. This territory in Western Australia was of great sacred significance to the Wunambal people because of ancient laws and traditions known as Wanjina-Wunggurr.

George adored his beloved sunburnt country and took great pride in playing tour guide. "You see, the Wanjina are the creator gods. They came from the wind and made everything from the Earth. They are responsible for all creation and regeneration. As such, their laws must be kept sacred; otherwise they could bring floods, cyclones and all kinds of natural disasters.

"The Wunggurr are the creation snakes. They make sure that the waters flow and there are plenty of good rains. They show themselves as rainbows in the mist over the waterfalls during the wet season. As these beings traveled over the land, we believe they left their shadows as paintings on the rocks. Come on, I'll show ya!" George said excitedly.

As he gracefully glided across the rocks on the red soil, Angel Ariel couldn't see any separation between George's feet and the ground. Her heart sensed a deep connection and reverence to his ancient land. Giggling out loud, she innocently said, "I don't know why I'm saying this, but your movements across the rock remind me of a lizard."

Smiling, George replied, "You got a keen eye, Missy. Me animal totem's a lizard."

"What's an animal totem?"

George was surprised by her question. "Struth, everyone is connected to a certain animal through life to help them grow and learn. Let me explain. Now you see here, me animal totem, the lizard, is all about the dream world beyond space and time. He kinda foretells the future. Because he has future vision, he always knows what will happen in advance, so this here lizard teaches us how to use our dreams to create a future reality. For instance, you can dream of something, but then it is up to the dreamer to decide whether to make it real or not.

"Lizard teaches us to be responsible for every single event in our lives, because everything that happens springs from either our wishes or our fears. He's a pretty clever little bloke."

"Hmmm", said Angel Ariel, "all that from a little lizard." She then became quite excited. "Tell me, George, do you know what my animal totem is?"

Staring deeply at her, George's head began to nod. "Caw mate, yer an easy one to read. No doubt you're a raven."

A look of horror swept across Angel Ariel's face. "That's horrible! Don't ravens eat dead animals?"

George laughed. "Yeah, that's true, but they're great recyclers! They do a good job cleanin' up nature's leftovers. But you know, ravens are also great communicators and real good at tellin' others where to find a good feed. Yet these smart little buggers don't just nourish our bodies, they also nourish our Spirit.

"Their black color and diet of dead animals makes people think about death, which is our unconscious. They help us change our perception and go within to connect with our multidimensional self and to reunite with the mysteries of the universe." George leaned closer to Angel Ariel and whispered, "Ravens are the 'keepers of secrets' and the teachers of magic."

Pausing for a moment, George wagged his finger at Angel Ariel and said, "No doubt you've had a history of pushing and prodding others to reunite with their higher selves. Am I right?"

Angel Ariel quickly remembered her lives as Annabel Rose, the healer, and Wachinksapa, the Medicine Man. Grinning, she agreed. "I guess you could say that I have done that a few times in my past."

"Sure enough and no doubt you'll keep on encouraging others to open up," George said deliberately. "It's just in your nature."

On their journey, they passed through large creeks and rivers that were lined with eucalyptus trees. George noticed that Angel Ariel was tiring in the hot conditions and he suggested a break in their journey. Stopping alongside one of the naturally-formed pools, they took shelter under some shady trees. Angel Ariel was treated to a colorful display of beautiful purple fairy wrens, rosellas and yellow wagtails as they adorned the trees with their vivid colors.

As she cupped her hands together to draw some cool water, she took a sip and looked at the lovely yellow acacia and red grevillea flowers against a backdrop of pandanus trees. The sights and sounds of this ancient land seemed vaguely familiar to Angel Ariel, and they began to reignite and stir deep feelings. George anxiously watched from a distance, as he knew this area would awaken long-held memories that had been locked away and dormant within Angel Ariel for such a long time.

All of a sudden, a wallaby bolted out of the forest and bounded right in front of her. This huge fright was enough to jolt her back in time; to when she and Kiel lived as Aborigines in the Kimberley some thirty-two thousand years ago. As if looking through a magical window, she was amazed to see a vision of herself and Kiel, along with their sixteen children, being the caretakers of a sacred well on this ancient land.

She watched in amazement as she taught her children where to find food and how to prepare it. Surrounded by her family, she felt a profound sense of belonging to this ancient land. This connection grew even deeper as she saw herself following the sacred laws and traditions that were established by the ancestral beings.

Unbeknownst to Angel Ariel, George had been silently observing her visions the whole time. He let out a huge laugh and slapped his knee. "Ha, I knew you was one of us! I recognized the light that was glowing about you. It reminded me of our ancestral beings—the ancient ones—who came from the stars and first taught us about the Dreamtime."

Angel Ariel was confused. "But how can that be? I'm not black."

George laughed as he stood up. "And neither were the first visitors to come to Australia. Let's keep movin' and I'll tell you about the white star people."

As they began their descent into the gorge, George paused as he gathered his thoughts. "You see, at the center of all Aboriginal life is the belief in the oneness of the spiritual, human and natural world. The

Dreaming or spiritual world runs through every part of our lives. It began at the dawn of time, is in the present moment and will last forever.

"When the Ancient Beings created everything of the land, sea and sky, they also created sacred rules and laws of culture, traditions and social life. This system that they passed down was complete in every way. They gave certain groups custodianship over the land; but only on the condition that they followed the laws. To make sure that those laws are correctly followed, the Ancient Beings have retained the ability to influence present-day lives. In this way, they are assured that the Aboriginal people will take responsibility and look after the land."

As they approached the bottom of the gorge, George continued, "We believe that our ancestors came from the stars. In fact, as far as us Aboriginals are concerned, what goes on in the heavens rules us. Just as Christians believe in Jesus and teachings like *Judge ye not that ye be judged yourself* and *Do unto others, that you would have them do unto you*, we believe in planetary saints or E.T.s. For thousands of years, we have called them Wandjiinas that came from the stars."

Quizzically, Angel Ariel asked, "If you are so connected to the land and your traditions, how do you know about Christian ways?"

George hesitated as the laughing note in his voice quickly disappeared, and he became quite somber. "Oh well, it's a bit of a sore point. As a young fella of twelve I was rounded up and taken away from me Mum and brothers and had to live in a mission far, far away."

"I'm sorry. You must have been so sad."

Picking up a rock and hurling it into the river, George replied, "I can tell you, Missy, it was no picnic. I was taken away from the only life I had ever known—me family. I felt as if me guts had been ripped out." Picking up another rock and skipping it along the water, George continued, "After bumping around in a car for days, we fronted up to a Catholic mission, where there were lots of Aboriginal children just like meself. But bloody hell, if it wasn't strange to see them in white man's clothing. I was forced to put clothes on and wear these bloody awful uncomfortable shoes. I couldn't feel the ground b'neath me feet and it was so itchy and stinkin' hot in them clothes.

"I tried to speak me own language with the other kids, but they would yell at me and tell me that I had to learn to speak English from now on. They forced us to learn and recite things from the Bible; tellin' us that the sacred laws and traditions that we learned from the Ancient Beings was rubbish and wrong. They told us that the right way was to believe in a new God, Jesus and all. One of the things they told us was to *consider the lilies* and how, if we believed in Jesus, we would have whatever we needed.

"But I told them that the Ancient Beings had already provided us with everything we could ever want from the land. They also said to follow rules like *love thy neighbor*. I knew that the Ancient Ones had already given us sacred rules on how to get along with one another thousands of years before 'this' religion came along. And anyway, I figured that if this was the way they showed love, by wrenching a young boy away from his family, well, I didn't want to have a bar of it.

"After a few months, I waited for a moonless night, ditched the clothes and shoes, and ran all the way back home. From that day forth, I learned from the Shaman how to be invisible and bloody well never got caught again."

As if he needed to quickly cut off that painful memory, George said, "You ready to have a look at the paintings?"

As George lead her around a bend, the indented rocks on the side of the gorge created small caves. As the paintings came into view, Angel Ariel looked on in amazed silence. The forms painted on the walls were strange, elongated beings with round, hairless heads and huge pools of dark eyes. A tiny speck seemed to represent a nose, yet there were no mouths drawn on the figures. Angel Ariel quickly intuited that because they had mastered the ability to speak telepathically, there was no need for them to have a mouth.

Most of the bald heads were surrounded by glowing, round helmets and the outline of the helmets looked as if they were generating some power source. Angel Ariel giggled as she thought perhaps that's what was making them look so bug-eyed.

Although the figures were of different shapes and sizes, they

169

all had huge eyes and wore their helmets of light. She also noticed paintings of strange disk-like objects that may have represented ancient flying crafts.

George broke the silence. "You know, it doesn't matter how many times I see them, it always stirs something really deep within me."

Still riveted by the paintings, Angel Ariel said, "I would love to know more about where they came from."

George jumped in with his reply. "Well, Missy, the story goes that long ago, way back in the Dreamtime, a great silver bird flew down from the sky. It tried to land safely on the ground but failed, and it broke apart. Out of the great silver bird from the stars came white-skinned gods and their children. With this Planet being so different from where they came from, the older Star Gods died off, 'cause they couldn't get used to the Earth. Yet their children were young and able to adapt to their new surroundings.

"In loving memory, the children painted their parents' likenesses on the cave walls. Over time, that big silver bird rusted away and eventually its red rust created the red soil of land.

"As time went by, the children who came from the sky increased in numbers and their white skins turned black to protect them from the harsh sun. These Star Gods taught about the Dreamtime knowledge. This knowledge of things far beyond our own visible dimension was handed down through the Aboriginal Shaman and Medicine Men."

Angel Ariel interrupted, "Were these the same men who taught you the gift of invisibility?"

"Yup," George said, "'zactly the same. These men of high magic have an ability to have out-of-body journeys and go to strange realms to meet the Sky Gods. Once there, they learn Star People knowledge. This ability to be able to travel through time is common among Medicine Men."

Upon the mention of Medicine Men and out-of-body journeys, Angel Ariel excitedly told George that when she was Wachinksapa, the Medicine Man of the Lakota, she took others out of physical space and time on vision quests to experience the dimension of Great Spirit.

Nodding his head in agreement, George continued, "Just like you did, they can go through the clouds and travel to other dimensions. Some white folks have experienced the same exact thing but aren't aware of it."

Watching Angel Ariel's confused expression, George explained, "How many people have talked about a beam of white light and felt themselves lifting through the air, up in the sky? They feel drawn to travel towards this beam of light through a tunnel as they enter a different dimension. Sounds pretty much the same to me, don't it?"

Changing the subject, George rubbed his stomach and announced, "I could sure go for some tucker. How about you?"

"Some what??"

"Oh yeah," said George. "Tucker, that means food." Opening up his kangaroo skin pouch, he took out some sandwiches.

Surprised, Angel Ariel quickly said, "Aren't you supposed to hunt and find the food?"

Smiling a cheeky grin, George replied, "Well, sometimes it's just easier to manifest a sandwich, eh?"

They ate in silence for a long time and listened to the whirring sounds of insects in the hot, dry air. Preempting her question, George said, "Go on and ask me."

Angel Ariel laughed as she had been thinking to ask George about his journeys through the window of time. "Well, I have been wondering, what's it like to be a multi-dimensional traveler?"

George took a long drink of water before explaining. "I know you've only experienced the seven dimensions of Heaven surrounding Earth, and haven't gone further than that yet. You know how, when a person dies, they transition through the tunnel and to the light, into the dimension of Heaven?"

Angel Ariel rolled her eyes. "Well, of course I know that."

"Well, we don't have to die in order to remove ourselves from this Earth dimension to enter another one. Through our ability to raise our energies and vibrations, we are able to disappear like the great Shaman."

"So what do they look like, these dimensions beyond Heaven?"

"You know, you may not believe it, but other dimensions have similar conditions to our world. It's kind of like a parallel Earth that has its own suns, moons and planets, with all kinds of life forms—although things like cities, transportation and science are much more advanced than what we know on this planet." George stopped for a moment and just shook his head. "It's so bloody vast that you can't even imagine it."

George took a big bite and finished his sandwich. "But you know what? The greatest difference between Earth and many of the other planets and dimensions is that they have transcended wars, hatred, racism and judgment. Yep, our inter-dimensional brothers and sisters live in peace, acceptance and harmony. They know that we are all One."

They sat for a while in silence, as Angel Ariel's thoughts raced with the infinite possibilities of the vastness of space and the prospect of one day meeting her inter-dimensional neighbors.

Packing up for the journey back, George added, "Earth is such a tiny speck of dust that sits on the edge of the Milky Way. People know so little about what and who else exists in the Universe. But the time is coming when we shall be made to take notice."

Climbing onto the path out of the gorge, Angel Ariel said, "So you think the Star People will try to contact us soon?"

"They already tried to make contact with us," George quickly replied, "but weren't welcomed and were met with complete fear and denial of their existence. There have been many cover-ups, too. Even the names 'science fiction' and 'aliens' that humans use in reference to Star People, it is so bloody offensive to those of us who know about and have experienced other worlds. Earth's stubborn viewpoint is that it is the only planet with intelligent life."

Unable to contain himself, George let out a huge belly laugh and wiped his eyes. "That's so ridiculous because I believe our inter-dimensional neighbors have been responsible for the creation of much of Earth's intelligent life. Many indigenous tribes have known this throughout time."

"So how do they create life on Earth?" questioned Angel Ariel.

"Well it's like this—they select certain individuals to be pre-programmed before birth to receive important knowledge and information for the advancement of the Earth. Certain people stand out from the rest of ordinary thinkers and creators. Fellas like Da Vinci and Bach and that science bloke Einstein, each of them were chosen to bring light to areas of the planet at a certain time in history."

Angel Ariel was listening intently as George continued, "Now here is the part that you can relate to. The Star People, with their ability to be invisible, are unseen guides to these particular people and help them towards success. People sense them as an unseen presence behind or beside them, often directing and guiding them away from dangerous situations. A lot of people refer to them as Spirit Guides."

"It's exactly the same as angels who help individuals bring forth exceptional creative intelligence," Angel Ariel quickly offered. "It is often perceived as a quiet voice that whispers ideas and thoughts to them. For instance, the music that I created while I was in Heaven was channeled to a young musician on Earth by his spirit guide. He did not know how he created it; and he said that he felt like the hand of God had given it to him.

"And while angels and spirit guides can't interfere with people's free will and free choice, humans recognize their gentle prodding through their intuition or sixth sense. Many times, that stroke of inspiration or genius was a direct result of an angel whispering in their ear."

George placed a friendly hand on her shoulder. "It just shows, you and me, we're workin' off the same page."

As Angel Ariel nodded her head in agreement, she suddenly felt a change in the air. With a knowing tone in his voice, George replied, "Seems like a willy-willy is blowin' and that's my cue to get goin'."

Perplexed, Angel Ariel said, "A willy-what-ty??"

"A willy-willy. It's a big funnel of wind that sucks up dust as it travels along; sort of like a small tornado." George held out his weathered, black hand and gently touched Angel Ariel's white cheek.

The stark contrast in their coloring gave even more power to the words he was about to speak. Smiling affectionately, George said, "Take what you've learned here and help others recognize and respect the gifts and traditions of all people. Whether it is faeries, animals, Aboriginals or Star People, our strength and ability to survive as a planet will have nothin' to do with emphasizing our differences and everything to do with the ability to recognize what makes us similar on the inside."

Watching as the strange funnel of dust steadily approached, George reached out into thin air, opened up an envelope of space and time, crawled through it and slipped out of sight.

Angel Ariel watched as the advancing willy-willy stopped right in front of her and continued to spin and turn on the spot. As her eyes were fixed on the long funnel of dust, her attention was quickly diverted by a sharp, high-pitched sound. She then recognized a familiar voice.

"You know, that noise has been trying to get my attention as well."

As the willy-willy stopped spinning and disappeared, her beloved Kiel stepped out of it. Overjoyed to see her Twin Flame, they embraced tenderly and touched their faces gently together. As their loving energies connected, their increased vibrations started to manifest and reveal their new destination.

14

Heaven—Ascension and the New Age of Aquarius

Standing on top of grand Mt. Tibrogargan, Angel Ariel and Kiel gazed in wonderment as the beauty of the Sunshine Coast, Australia, appeared in front of them. Lush green fields of sugar cane rolled out before them and were quickly contrasted by the shimmering blue expanse of the Pacific Ocean. The beautiful sight was like a present from God; wrapped up with a ribbon of white sandy beaches that hugged the shoreline.

Dotting the landscape and rising over 1,800 feet was the Glass House Mountains. These volcanic eruptions, also known as the Guardians of the Dreamtime, were of sacred significance to the Aboriginal people. It was the combination of the sea and these ancient mountains that gave this stretch of coastline extraordinarily high energies. From this grand vantage point, Angel Ariel and Kiel feasted on the vast, shining blue water and basked in the golden rays of the late afternoon sun.

With dusk quickly approaching, the Twin Flames turned their thoughts to manifesting their treasured beachside home. Made of stone, wood and glass, it married all the natural elements and was a reflection of nature's beauty all around them. The skylights and large windows brought in the fresh sea breeze on all sides. A large glass atrium in the center of the home, with its fountain, bamboo plants and soft, white pebbles, gave the house a Japanese feel. The soothing sound of the cascading water from the fountain, and the continual flow of peaceful energies within the home created an atmosphere of hushed tranquility.

As the last pieces of furniture manifested to complete their sacred sanctuary, Angel Ariel remembered one of her favorite things to do. Hurrying to the kitchen, she grabbed some slices of bread and headed out the back door. Sitting in the garden, she was surrounded by an array of native plants. The deep red bottlebrushes, kangaroo paw and golden wattles encouraged the birds to feed and come find peace in the quiet, safe haven of their backyard.

She loved entertaining the endless stream of feathered visitors: black and white magpies, willy wagtails, lorikeets and cockatoos. And although she did love them all equally, she had to admit that her heart skipped a beat when the cheeky kookaburras came to call. Their perpetual smiles and happy song made Angel Ariel laugh and reminded her not to take life too seriously.

The Twin Flames had made a pact that whenever they were together and not separated by Earthly incarnations, they would share God's beautiful nightly show and watch the sunset together. The last rays of the golden sunset had dipped from sight and lines of soft pastel pink and lavender hues now painted the sky.

As the stars began to pop through the fading pink, the first tinges of blue washed the heavens. Watching the full moon rise to take its place in the blue of the evening sky, the Twin Flames could hear the waves lapping against the shoreline.

The rhythmic sound provided a soothing lullaby for both of them. Gently touching their faces together, they enfolded into each other's arms and peacefully drifted off to sleep.

With the first light of dawn, they were jolted from their sleep by the high-pitched, piercing sound that they had both heard the day before. Arising quickly, they followed in the direction of the sound. Wending their way through the paper bark forest that ran along the sand dunes, they stepped out of the forest onto a beach of white, powdery sand. The urgent sound seemed to be pulling them closer to the ocean's edge. Immediately, both Kiel and Angel Ariel realized that it was the familiar song of their dolphin friends.

Tuning in to the dolphin's sonar frequencies, Angel Ariel asked them to come closer to the shore. As she looked out to sea, she watched a huge wave start to form in the distance. As the wave advanced closer to the shore and was about to crest, a pod of dolphins appeared in the crystal clear waters, reuniting them once again with their cherished friends.

Speaking as a single group, the dolphins focused on her mind. In return, Angel Ariel was able to communicate by focusing on one dolphin. "It is so wonderful to be with you once again, Manakel."

Smiling with deep, inner wisdom, Manakel telepathically connected with her. "We are so excited to see both of you once more. The reason for our call of alarm was to alert you to the urgency of raising Earth's energies. This is of great importance in order for Earth and all her inhabitants to ascend into the Age of Aquarius. And it is for this reason that my request to be your third guide was granted."

Angel Ariel's heart filled with joy at this realization that her cherished friend had requested to be her next guide.

"We are delighted that our efforts of channeling the messages of unconditional love are finally starting to be accepted by many people. This has caused a shift in the energetic make-up of the Planet; from one of lower, dense vibrations to those of light and love. Thankfully, we have not been alone in our efforts and have had many glorious light beings like you to show others how to live in peace, harmony, non-judgment and acceptance."

Nodding her head in agreement, Angel Ariel replied, "There are so many light workers scattered far and wide across this beautiful planet who work tirelessly to rid the Earth of wars, hatred and man's inhumanity to man. Manakel, you, along with many other cetaceans, work tirelessly to hold this light of peace. What more can we do to help increase your loving efforts?"

The dolphin spoke solemnly, "Living in love and harmony would provide the span for mankind to progress from existing in separation to living in unity. The more our individual and combined efforts exemplify this belief, the more it will trigger man to wake up to live in peace."

As he continued, Manakel's voice then took on a note of sadness. "This unity is the only thing that will allow all living things on the Earth to ascend as a species. The Earth has gotten to a point that she cannot absorb any more bloodshed, hatred and disregard for basic human rights. Our dolphin families have tried to offer the uplifting of Earth energies with our gift of sonar to support man's continued awakening. Traveling on our migratory paths, we often flow with and follow the needs of the Earth. In areas of hatred, war and indifference, our sonar has been able to cut through heavy pockets of negative energy, helping the lower frequencies to rise again once more. Yet this ability is not relegated solely to dolphins.

"Humans can begin to move their frequencies ever higher through choosing love, acceptance and forgiveness. In fact, we have seen a great shift in energy as people start to care deeply about what happens to their fellow man and their planet. Their heightened energies are causing a chain reaction of enlightenment throughout the Earth."

Taking a few moments to roll about in the beautiful turquoise waters, Manakel leapt high out of the water and came down with a huge splash. Surfacing once again, he smiled at his friends.

"All people need to do is to look to the dolphins for an example of living in joy and harmony. We work and play in total synchronicity with one another." Sounding a high-pitched dolphin laugh, he continued, "Perhaps that is why we have what appears to be a perpetual smile on our faces and the reason why so many people are drawn to swim with us. Their conscious minds may not recognize it, but their connectedness to their hearts—and to all other hearts—knows this deeply. They feel freed from the shackles of negativity and sadness and get swept away by our joy and unconditional love."

Diving out of sight and coming up with a fish in his mouth,

Manakel swallowed it. "All this talk is making me hungry." Then, with a sense of urgency in his voice, he said, "My beautiful friends Angel Ariel and Kiel, please stress to humans to communicate beyond their five senses and open their hearts to connect with each other and all of God's creatures."

As Manakel's family formed a circle around him, he once again spoke for the group. "We want to ask humans why they choose to focus on the negative things that happen and base the majority of their lives on this negativity. We want to stress to humans that they can change their perception of the past and choose to focus on positive things that happen. In this way, they can move forward in appreciation and gratitude."

Moving back into formation with the other dolphins, Manakel concluded, "For the sake of our planet's survival, humans must wake up to realize that it is only by living in harmony with oneself that they can start to live in harmony with all others outside of themselves. This not only includes all races, species and cultures on Earth, but inter-dimensionally as well.

"The fact is that we are not alone. Earth finds herself at a critical time in her ascension. It is of utmost importance for humans to wake up and acknowledge that there are other civilizations in the Universe. Whether the message comes from dolphins, our inter-dimensional neighbors or ancient tribes like the Aboriginals, the message is still the same. It is only through our ability to reach out in love and openness to all beings that we will find the peace and unity we are so desperately looking for."

The dolphins then turned in unison and headed out to sea. As Angel Ariel waved goodbye, she faintly heard them above the sound of the crashing waves. "We love you both. Thank you for your wonderful efforts to help our beautiful planet survive."

In that moment, she and Kiel realized that, instead of being at the end of their journey, all the spiritual wisdom and experiences that they had garnered from their many incarnations had been preparing them for this very moment.

With an excited tone in her voice, Angel Ariel said to Kiel, "Now I realize, Kiel, that when one is on the spiritual path, one is always at the beginning. Each new piece of knowledge and awakening is a doorway to ever-increasing wisdom and possibilities."

With eager enthusiasm, Angel Ariel held Kiel's hand and lovingly gazed into his eyes. "I just can't wait to see the next chapter that we are going to manifest."

THE END ...

... and the beginning.

Epilogue

Having discovered her '*One True Home*' and removed the 'Veil of Forgetfulness,' Angel Ariel transcended the karmic wheel of life and death and did not need to return for further incarnations to the physical world. She vowed to remain in Heaven and was happy to be in service to God as an angel and spiritual teacher. Yet, with the approach of the year 2000, people began to awaken and realize that the only way that planet Earth would be able to survive was if its inhabitants lived in harmony and acceptance.

By choosing to raise their consciousness, many people in the world were shifting their lower, negative vibrations of fear, hatred, greed and control to higher, positive vibrations of peace, love, truth and unity. By holding these higher vibrations, they were bringing more light to the Earth. These spiritual warriors of love have been called 'Light Workers.'

As the Earth was ascending to higher, more light-filled vibrations, it was critical for each Light Worker to hold and emanate the energies of love and acceptance. Knowing how important it was for as many individuals as possible to hold light within in order to increase the light of love for the planet, Angel Ariel decided to incarnate one more time to help hold the light.

One True Home was the foundation of Angel Ariel's journey and will continue in my next book, *My One True Home*.

You will read how Angel Ariel combined the wisdom learned from her spiritual lessons and incarnated once more to be that spiritual guide and teacher to help others remember their own Divine, eternal nature. Yet, as you will discover, the path to her next incarnation did not follow the usual death and birth cycle.

For you see, Angel Ariel contracted to be a Walk-In and experience an Angelic soul exchange. Through her Angelic Walk-In experience, she brought Heaven down to Earth for herself and many others. This incredible experience saw Angel Ariel being reunited with her Twin Flame, Kiel, on the Earth plane in order to bring forth a very important mission of God. Come discover the beginning of Angel Ariel's next extraordinary life, in my sequel, *My One True Home,* due for release, Spring 2016.

Love and Angel Blessings,
Claire Candy Hough

About the Author

As a writer and author, international radio host, inspirational speaker, Reiki Master/Teacher and an Angel Practitioner, Claire Candy Hough helps individuals raise their consciousness and reconnect to the Divine within. She established her business, Angel Healing House, www.angelhealinghouse.com, after her spiritual awakening and Walk-In experience in 2003.

As a healing practitioner, Claire Candy helps her clients transform their lives physically and emotionally through Reiki, a form of energy medicine. As a clairvoyant and intuitive counselor, she marries spiritual knowledge with very grounded and practical ways that people can live truthful lives and shine their authentic light to the world.

After establishing a community of light on the Sunshine Coast in beautiful Queensland, Australia, she and her Twin Flame, husband Pete, followed the voice of the Divine and moved to the United States in 2008. With her move to the Los Angeles area in 2010, Claire Candy has brought her enthusiasm, passion and joy as she helps others to live authentic lives and manifest their dreams.

Her beautiful channeled book, *Angels of Faith,* was published in 2009 and is based on her two near-death experiences. Claire Candy's beautiful guided angel meditation CD, *Letting Go of Concerns and Living in the NOW!,* takes the listener on a wonderful journey with the Angels that helps restore peace, balance and calm.

Claire Candy has appeared on television and radio in California and Australia and has designed several transformative workshops including:

The Twin Flame
Relationship Workshop

A Twin Flame is the only other person in any space, time or dimension who is the completion of who you are. When brought together, it is the original Divine representation of perfect love. This workshop addresses why you haven't yet drawn this beautiful love to yourself and the important, practical tools that you can consciously focus on to bring such a relationship to you.

"I would recommend Candy's 'Twin Flame Relationship Workshop' to anyone curious about making the right choices in their lives. Candy's presentation clearly demonstrated how our life's story is interrelated to our own belief system. She teaches through examples how each human being is born with an already built-in intuition and, by not honoring this inner wisdom, we can wreak havoc in our personal lives. Candy's approach to her teachings stems from her own personal life experience from her two near-death experiences and the chain of events that followed throughout her life. Her life's teachings have shown me how to appreciate my own unique ability in order to be the change I want to see and to have the courage and clarity to make the right decisions." Renee, Hollywood, CA

Love of Self – Connecting to the Divine Within

This workshop encourages participants to go on an exploration for hidden treasure. This priceless treasure is more valuable and more long-lasting than gold, silver or jewels. It is how to love ourselves. Once we connect with our Divine light within, we will have the clarity, peace and balance to then break the bonds of self-limitation and to reach our highest potential.

"Candy's workshops are extraordinary and transformative. She effortlessly weaves valuable, life-changing information into a highly original, entertaining, practical presentation. Her message of 'Connecting to the Divine Within' is delivered with great enthusiasm, humor and compassion. I came away feeling special and unique, and empowered to pursue my full potential. Thank you, Candy, for your wisdom and your 'Healing from the Heart.' You are truly an Earth angel helping to enlighten others." Peter, Santa Barbara, CA

Near-Death Experiences – An Early Glimpse of Our Journey Back Home

If you have ever wondered about death—and haven't we all at some stage or another?—come along for an enjoyable look at dying. Having had two near-death experiences, Claire Candy remembers vividly her remarkable journey across the veil with the angels and the spiritual insights that she was shown in order to show others to 'not be so afraid of the dark.'

This informative talk will weave Claire Candy's personal near-death experiences with medical and scientific research by eminent doctors in the near-death field like Dr. Elizabeth Kubler-Ross, Dr. Raymond Moody, P.M.H.Atwater and Dr. Kenneth Ring. With humor, great reverence, compassion and love, she is able to make this subject not only enjoyable, but something to look forward to!!

"Candy Hough is an enlightened being, and her journey to that transformation in consciousness through two near-death experiences is shared with warmth, humor and great insight in her presentation entitled, 'Near Death Experiences—An Early Glimpse of Our Journey Back Home.' Candy seamlessly blends well-researched documentation of the near death experience with her own fascinating experience of this life-affirming, life-changing event. You will come away inspired, touched and with a new awareness of that most fascinating of all journeys. It is the best presentation on this topic that I have ever seen."

Reverend Terri Cooper, M.A., MFT, Santa Barbara, CA

Future Titles by
Claire Candy Hough

My One True Home

Love of Self—Connecting to the Divine Within

Twin Flame Relationships

The Posse of Angels—Wisdom from Angel Healing House

The Gift of Fate

Fish in the Sea

The Magic within You

CPSIA information can be obtained
at www.ICGtesting.com
Printed in the USA
FSOW01n0637130715
8743FS